Education and the Value of Knowledge

Introductory Studies in Philosophy of Education
Series Editors: PHILIP SNELDERS and COLIN WRINGE

Education and the Value of Knowledge by
M. A. B. Degenhardt

Can We Teach Children To Be Good by
Roger Straughan

Means and Ends in Education by Brenda Cohen

Education and the Value of Knowledge

M. A. B. DEGENHARDT

Department of Educational Studies,
The University of Tasmania

London
GEORGE ALLEN & UNWIN
Boston   Sydney

**George Allen & Unwin (Publishers) Ltd,
40 Museum Street, London WC1A 1LU, UK**

George Allen & Unwin (Publishers) Ltd,
Park Lane, Hemel Hempstead, Herts HP2 4TE, UK

Allen & Unwin, Inc.,
9 Winchester Terrace, Winchester, Mass. 01890, USA

George Allen & Unwin Australia Pty Ltd,
8 Napier Street, North Sydney, NSW 2060, Australia

First published in 1982

British Library Cataloguing in Publication Data

Degenhardt, M. A. B.
    Education and the value of knowledge.—
(Introductory studies in philosophy of education)
1. Knowledge, Theory of—History
I. Title   II. Series
121   BD161

ISBN 0-04-370115-9
ISBN 0-04-370116-7 Pbk

Library of Congress Cataloging in Publication Data

Degenhardt, M. A. B.
    Education and the value of knowledge.
(Introductory studies in philosophy of education)
Includes bibliographical references and index.
1. Education—Philosophy.   2. Knowledge, Theory of.
I. Title.   II. Series.
LB1033.D43   370'.1   82-4044
ISBN 0-04-370115-9   AACR2
ISBN 0-04-370116-7 (pbk.)

Set in 11 on 12 point Plantin by Rowland Phototypesetting Ltd
Bury St Edmunds, and printed in Great Britain
by Richard Clay (The Chaucer Press) Ltd,
Bungay, Suffolk

Contents

Editors' Foreword

Books that are available to students of philosophy of education may, in general, be divided into two types. There are collections of essays and articles making up a more or less random selection; and there are books which explore a single theme or argument in depth but, having been written to break new ground, are often unsuitable for general readers or those near the beginning of their course. The Introductory Studies in Philosophy of Education are intended to fill what is widely regarded as an important gap in this range.

The series aims to provide a collection of short, readable works which, besides being philosophically sound, will seem relevant and accessible to future and existing teachers without a previous knowledge of philosophy or of philosophy of education. In the planning of the series account has necessarily been taken of the tendency of present-day courses of teacher education to follow a more integrated and less discipline-based pattern than formerly. Account has also been taken of the fact that students on three- and four-year courses, as well as those on shorter postgraduate and in-service courses, quite understandably expect their theoretical studies to have a clear bearing on their practical concerns, and on their dealings with children. Each book, therefore, starts from a real and widely recognised problem in the educational field, and explores the main philosophical approaches which illuminate and clarify it, or suggests a coherent standpoint even when it does not claim to provide a solution. Attention is paid to the work of both mainstream philosophers and philosophers of education. For students who wish to pursue particular questions in depth, each book contains a bibliographical essay or a substantial list of suggestions for further reading. It is intended that a full range of the main topics recently discussed by philosophers of education should eventually be covered by the series.

Besides having considerable experience in the teaching of philosophy of education, the majority of authors writing in the series have already received some recognition in their particular fields. In addition, therefore, to reviewing and criticising existing work, each author has his or her own positive contribution to make to further discussion.

In *Education and the Value of Knowledge* Dr Degenhardt deals with such all-important questions of curriculum justification as 'why do we value knowledge?'; 'why is it that we value some kinds of knowledge more than others?'; 'can we simply perceive knowledge to be good, or is our belief that it is so grounded in man's nature, or that of knowledge itself?'. Traditional theories of justification are examined, and there is detailed discussion of contributions to this question by such well-known philosophers as Hirst, Peters, Elliott and White.

In the final chapter Dr Degenhardt advances and defends his own suggestion that the dichotomy between instrumentally useful and intrinsically worthwhile knowledge is a false one, and that educationally valuable knowledge is that which gives meaning to the individual's life and enables him to determine his own ends.

PHILIP SNELDERS
COLIN WRINGE

Preface

This book considers one problem in the theory of education. It is intended as an introductory work and the bulk of it comes in Chapter 2, which surveys some of the main approaches to the problem that have been suggested. To attempt to cover such a range of thinkers and theorists in a few pages is inevitably to risk distortions and misrepresentation. So the book is likely to do positive harm in so far as it is read as anything other than an introduction and invitation to a study of the originals. The problem considered has to do with different kinds of knowledge and their value. I have treated the arts as an area of knowledge without facing up to questions about whether they are, and in what sense. However, this will, I hope, emphasise the importance of such questions to educational theory.

I wish to thank former colleagues at Stockwell College of Education (now unfortunately closed) and present colleagues at the University of Tasmania: formal and informal discussions with them have enriched and clarified my thinking on the issues discussed. I am particularly grateful to Miss Vicki Raymond and Miss Joy McRae for their help in checking manuscripts and typescripts and to Mrs Cate Lowry for typing the text with great speed and efficiency.

I

Introduction: The Problem and Why It Matters

In educating people we try either to teach them something, or to encourage them to learn for themselves. What is to be learned may be straightforward facts, or it may be skills, attitudes, habits, beliefs, and so on. Whichever is the case, the attempt is to change people in some way. This being so, education must involve judgements about what sort of changes are desired. This is true for 'traditionalists' passing on knowledge from above and for 'progressivists' encouraging active growth from within. Either way, value judgements must be made regarding what to pass on or what growth to foster. Lively debate is likely to ensue. This book considers just one aspect of what is involved in deciding what to teach: one aspect of the problem of curriculum justification.

The problem is big and complex, and two aspects must be kept in mind here, though they can only be explored in companion volumes. First, there is the question of who ought to choose the curriculum. It is hard to decide between such powerful claimants as teachers, parents, priests, students, employers, politicians and pupils. This question is related to, but distinct from, the question to be considered here: whether there can be grounds for choosing a curriculum that are valid regardless of who does the choosing. Secondly, there is the question of what it is useful to learn. Most people would agree that we should teach children things that are likely to be useful in later life: useful to the individual or to his community. So the curriculum should include items that will in time help pupils to earn a living, run a home, fulfil obligations as citizens, and so on. But deciding what will be useful for children to learn is doubly difficult. It is partly a problem of predicting their future lives, and partly a problem of principle. For in judging what will be useful for someone we are also making judgements about how he ought to live. This is why there are protests when schools teach different 'useful' things to children of different sexes or social groups, thereby preparing them for different roles and opportunities.

However, not everything taught in school is taught because it is useful, and the aspect of the problem of curriculum justification to be considered in this book arises as follows. We might agree that an education is deficient if it omits the following: scientific explanations of the natural world, the human past, literature and art, another language and culture, different religions and ideologies that men have lived by, systematic investigations of human thought, conduct and institutions and advanced mathematics. For we might find knowledge of such things valuable and believe that it should be taught in schools; and we might back up this belief with rather vague talk of 'culture', 'higher learning', 'worthwhile activities', 'serious pursuits', 'realm of intellect', and so on. But in urging the value of such knowledge we would be unwise to claim that it is useful. Certainly for a few pupils much of such knowledge may indeed turn out to be useful in later life: if, say, they earn a living as scientific researchers, archaeologists, priests, or journalists. And for many more pupils odd items of such knowledge may turn out to be useful: helping them, say, to recognise Athens when they go on holiday, to spot a disease, to win a TV quiz show, or to pick up a Velázquez at a jumble sale. But it can hardly be claimed that such bodies of knowledge are generally useful to everyone. So if they are indeed worthy of study by people in general this must be on account of something other than their usefulness. The difficulty, though, is to see what this something else can be: to see what justifies the use of labour, resources and perhaps coercion to teach children things that are unlikely to be useful. This is the problem with which this book is concerned.

A common solution says that such non-useful knowledge has

a different kind of value, that it is valuable not because it is useful or a means to some further end, but because it is an end in itself: it is intrinsically rather than instrumentally good. Some critics reply that such talk is really a disguised admission of inability to argue the case for the 'higher learning'. Defenders reply that it cannot be the case that all human goods are instrumental goods, or means to further goods. For then we would have a most peculiar state of affairs in which X is only good because it leads on to Y, and Y in turn is only good because it leads on to Z, and so on to infinity: in which case the whole business could hardly have got started. It seems that if there are to be any goods in the world, then some things must simply be goods in themselves. Thus it might be agreed that happiness is intrinsically good: that it just *is* a good thing for people to be happy regardless of whether this happiness leads on to other things.

If this argument is correct, then intrinsic goods seem to be superior to instrumental goods. For something that is good as a means to some further end just happens to be good in certain circumstances. It only acquires its goodness from some more fundamental intrinsic good to which it is a means. While something that is good in itself is good regardless of circumstance.

Given, then, that knowledge is often an instrumental good, can it be maintained that some, perhaps all, knowledge is also one of the ultimate intrinsic goods? In due course we will see that this suggestion raises several serious difficulties, one of which must be stated at once. If we are to say that some knowledge is a good in itself we need to be able to specify the marks or characteristics of such knowledge, and to find reasons for finding it intrinsically valuable. Otherwise we may be arbitrarily claiming some absolute and inscrutable value for mere personal preferences. Yet it is difficult to see what kinds of grounds could be given for finding some or all knowledge intrinsically valuable. For by definition a claim to intrinsic value cannot be backed up by reference to extrinsic usefulness. In other words, to be able to talk of knowledge as intrinsically valuable we must be able to show grounds for valuing it without making any reference to the use to which that knowledge might be put, or to other advantages it might yield.

3

Theorists have often grappled with this problem, and Chapter 2 will explore the main *kinds* of answers they have proposed. The problem being a perennial one, reference will be to past and present thinkers. But as we are not studying the history of ideas, answers will be grouped according to kind of argument rather than chronology. We shall first consider the views of intuitionist theorists who believe that the value of something is a self-evident objective property 'intuitable' by any clear, unprejudiced mind. Then we shall consider 'naturalistic' arguments according to which certain values follow from the nature of man: the several versions of this argument embodying different views of man's nature. Next we shall look at arguments from the nature of knowledge rather than man, and conclude the survey by considering the possibility of a religious answer. Finding difficulties with all these approaches we will see why some theorists believe it impossible and/or undesirable for educators to make judgements about the value or educational worth of knowledge. Such a view, however, could be damaging to education, and Chapter 3 will propose a positive argument whereby knowledge is valuable in a way that takes us beyond a simple dichotomy between extrinsic and intrinsic value.

All this may sound like arid theorising best ignored by busy teachers, so something must now be said about why our problem is among the most urgent and practical of all educational questions.

First, any teacher is likely to be challenged as to the worth of what he teaches. The challenge may come from a bored pupil who sees no point in history; from a parent who wants his children to get job qualifications rather than study astronomy; from a practically minded headmaster who does not like poetry. It is not easy to find answers to satisfy these questioners, and the thoughtful teacher will feel the need for answers to satisfy himself in face of the doubts they raise. They may, after all, be right: perhaps it *is* a mistake to require pupils to partake of the 'high culture' of non-useful knowledge. A teacher troubled by such misgivings may lose confidence and enthusiasm for his work, or seek a compromise by teaching his subjects so as to make them more 'useful'. But horrible barbarisms and corruptions can arise when the teacher of a subject with its own worth

4

and coherence tries to make it 'useful' or 'relevant' by artificially linking it to the exigencies of daily life.

These questions may also arise when we reflect on how we educate ourselves. Anxious to improve and inform our own minds, but unable to study everything, we may ask what is most worth knowing about and why. We may even wonder if we should spend *any* time and energy on self-education when we might be boozing or campaigning for social justice.

The problem arises again at the level of overall educational planning when teachers and others design courses of study. Indeed, it may be here that those who value the 'high culture' are most likely to lose out against those who care only for useful learning. Anti-intellectualist attitudes are often influential, and in education they can pass as enlightened and humane. Consider, for example, the appeal and impact of the Newsom Committee's view that education makes sense if it is practical, realistic and vocational (Newsom, 1963, ch. 14). And in an era of educational economy the non-useful is at risk.

These considerations render one kind of answer to our problem simply inadequate. Challenged to show the intrinsic value of medieval studies or astrophysics, we may incline to say that if someone gets 'into' these subjects in the right way he may or may not find them valuable: but if he does not then there is nothing more to say. There is much to be said for this view: perhaps beauty, knowledge and understanding simply are things you either do or do not value regardless of any amount of argument. Unfortunately, such a position is necessarily without persuasive power: for it involves saying that if I value something and want to include it in the curriculum, then I can say nothing to change the feelings of those who disagree. So there are reasons of strategy as well as principle for seeking more positive justifications.

There is one further point. The reason why we teach something makes a difference to how we teach it and thereby to how we organise schools, educate teachers, use examinations, and so on.

Summary of Chapter 1

Some knowledge seems to deserve a place in the curriculum, though not because it is useful. It is thought to be intrinsically rather than instrumentally good. For several reasons it is important to work out just what knowledge is good in this way, and why.

(1) We cannot teach or study everything. Some selection has to be made.
(2) Why we teach something may determine how we teach it.
(3) Teachers need to be able to answer reasonable critics and to feel confident of the worth of what they are teaching.
(4) Some people would like to confine the curriculum to what is useful. If they are wrong they must be answered. But –
(5) They may be right.

2

Some Theories of the Inherent Worth of Knowledge

I Intuitionist Theories

Notwithstanding the arguments of Chapter 1, readers may still doubt the point of this inquiry. They may care so much for their own discipline that to ask for proof of its worth sounds like some philistine affront: the call for a *proof* of the worth of physics or poetry can only come from one who is blind to their worth. The value of these activities is simply *there*, lying *in them* and waiting to be seen. Education may help someone to see such value more clearly: nothing more can or should be attempted.

To think this is, perhaps inadvertently, to align oneself with the philosophical doctrine of ethical intuitionism, according to which ultimate values are objective, but not a matter for argument or proof. Rather, the good and the bad are objectively known because they are intuited. We need no arguments to show that human creativity is desirable or that wanton cruelty is undesirable: we just *know* that one is good and the other bad.

Two points must be stressed if we are to avoid misunderstanding intuitionism. First, the claim that our intuitions give us objective knowledge is not a claim about subjective feelings or personal preferences. Secondly, intuitionism need not postulate some mysterious power of knowing, or non-sensory perception. Rather it holds that, unless things go wrong, we can all know what things are good and bad because their goodness or badness are self-evident qualities to be seen by all.

It will be helpful to attend to an influential version of ethical intuitionism expounded by G. E. Moore in his *Principia Ethica* (Moore, 1960 [1903]). As a philosopher Moore reflects not on individual moral problems but on the ultimate basis of our moral understanding. Here he thinks there are two questions.

(1) What kinds of things ought to exist for their own sakes?
(2) What kinds of actions ought we to perform?

The answers to (1), he believes, can be known by intuition and only by intuition. These answers, in turn, enable us to work out the answers to (2): for if some states of affairs ought to exist for their own sakes, then we ought to do the things most likely to bring about such states. This sets Moore apart from most intuitionists who have believed that our duties (or what things we ought to do) are self-evident, and it makes his theory more clearly relevant to our present concern with what knowledge is good in itself.

Moore thinks that the goodness of intrinsically good things can be recognised but not defined. This is because good is a simple, unanalysable property. There are two kinds of things in the world: simple things like colours which cannot be analysed into components, and complex things like horses which can (legs, heart, liver, and so on). Goodness belongs to the first kind. 'Yellow and good, we say, are not complex: they are notions of that simple kind out of which definitions are composed and with which the power of further defining ceases' (Moore, 1960, p. 8). Such indefinability, however, need not trouble us; for we can recognise the goodness of something just as we can recognise its yellowness. Certainly we can sometimes be confused here: for it is not always clear whether something which is good is intrinsically good, or good as a means to something else. Moore suggests we guard against such confusion and focus our attention on the intrinsic goodness of something by 'considering what value we should attach to it, if it existed in absolute isolation, stripped of all its usual accompaniments' (ibid., p. 91).

Once apply this method of 'absolute isolation' and, Moore confides, the answer to questions about what things are good in themselves becomes pleasingly simple.

8

By far the most valuable things, which we know or can imagine, are certain states of consciousness, which may be roughly described as the pleasures of human intercourse and the enjoyment of beautiful objects. No one, probably, who has asked himself the question, has ever doubted that personal affection and the appreciation of what is beautiful in Art or Nature, are good in themselves; nor, if we consider strictly what things are worth having *purely for their own sakes*, does it appear probable that anyone will think that anything else has *nearly* so great a value as the things which are included under these two heads. (ibid., pp. 188–9)

This brief and exclusive catalogue will give no cheer to educators seeking assurance that knowledge is intrinsically good, and Moore does go on to say that knowledge has 'little or no value by itself' (p. 199) though it is a constituent of the highest goods. We shall return to the important point that Moore's intuitions do not command the agreement he anticipates. However, it is often possible to learn from and follow a philosopher's methods without sharing all his conclusions, and one writer has recently used Moore's kind of approach to defend the intrinsic worth of knowledge and draw educational implications. In his paper 'Towards an axiology of knowledge' R. K. W. Paterson considers two questions:

First, what value should we attach to knowledge as such? Does knowledge figure, and how does it figure among those things – pleasure, justice, beauty, virtuous character and so on – which we consider to be of value in themselves, quite apart from any consequences they may have? Secondly, how can we establish the comparative value of different types and items of knowledge . . . ? (Paterson, 1979, pp. 91–2)

Regarding the first question, he points out that knowledge cannot be just one among other values like pleasure, justice, or beauty: for in one way or another all these values involve knowledge. But as well as such ancillary value he believes that knowledge does have its own intrinsic worth. To see this, he suggests we follow another ethical intuitionist, W. D. Ross, who also proposed a 'technique' for isolating the object of evaluation in order to make it the focus of our intuiting powers. The value of knowledge in its own right becomes evident if we imagine two states of the world exactly similar, except that in one the inhabitants had a far greater understanding of the laws of the universe. This 'thought experiment', it is claimed, leaves us in no doubt that the knowledgeable state would be better. This intuition fits in with our preference for truth over falsity and for conscious beings over inanimate objects: such considerations tending 'to show pretty conclusively that knowledge is something which ought to be valued for its own sake' (Paterson, 1979, p. 93).

But if knowledge as such is clearly of intrinsic worth, things are more difficult regarding Paterson's second question about the comparative worth of different items or areas of knowledge. He outlines four criteria to be brought to bear and weighed against each other.

(1) Pieces of knowledge have intrinsic worth in isolation: but they gain worth as parts of wider bodies of knowledge, contributing to a pattern of mutually explanatory and illuminating facts.

(2) Knowledge gains worth from the cognitive richness of its objects. There are things that are more worth knowing about because there is more to know about them on account of their magnitude or complexity.

(3) Knowledge gains worth by being about something that itself has worth. Thus knowledge about a particular work of art may rate low on (2) because of that work's stark simplicity but score highly on (3) because of its aesthetic merit.

(4) Knowledge can be more or less full and reliable. Thus theological knowledge would score highly on (1), (2) and (3); for it relates to all other knowledge, has a rich subject matter and aspires to tell us about something important. Yet it will score low on (4) because it is notoriously incomplete and unreliable.

Paterson explains these criteria very fully and stresses the need to weigh one against another. But he does not argue for them, presumably thinking that they are self-evident to any accurately focused intuition. (Readers may consult their own intuitions.) As for actually using these criteria to grade the comparative worths of different items or areas of knowledge, he finds the task prohibitively complex – made especially so by the shifting state of human knowledge. He contents himself with the general conclusion that, whatever their relative merits, the intrinsic cognitive importance of the basic forms of knowledge gives them precedence over lesser systems or units.

> Individual pieces of knowledge and specialised bodies of knowledge, however important, largely owe what importance they have to the light shed by our understanding of the forms of knowledge by which they are shaped and governed, and every advance we make in our understanding of one of the great forms of knowledge has a far-reaching, seismic significance for our grasp of the numberless pieces of knowledge and the many specialised bodies of knowledge which depend on it. Through the great forms of knowledge – mathematics, the physical sciences, the sciences of mind and society, philosophy and so on – we are given access to reality in its most fundamental features, we come to see something of its ground-plan, the master structures and principles of its workings, its key properties and their interrelations, and so ultimately our whole experience becomes charged with meaning at its deepest and most pervasive levels. (Paterson, 1979, pp. 97–8)

Now many may endorse this conclusion, but the question at stake is whether intuitionism provides an adequate justification for it. Having considered Moore's intuitionist theory of ethics and Paterson's use of intuitionism to tackle an educational problem, we must now face objections to their approach. Here it is important to bear in mind the central intuitionist claim: that truths about values are self-evidently true; so that, while the experience of intuiting them may be a subjective or personal experience, it is yet an intuition of something objective, of something there for anyone to see, provided he focuses his attention properly.

Two objections will occur to many readers.

(1) The intuitionist's claim seems to be incompatible with the diversity of views, between individuals and between cultures, as to which things are good or bad. Surely such striking disagreements would not arise if good and bad were objectively self-evident to all.

(2) Developments in psychology and sociology have shown us how differences in education and upbringing generate different world views and values. Perhaps some values seem self-evident and objective to us because we have been so thoroughly socialised that we do not even realise it: we think that opinions we have learned are truths evident to all.

Some philosophers think the intuitionist cannot meet such objections: but he does have points to make in reply. We have seen how Moore and Ross attribute many false judgements to lack of care in focusing attention on the object of appraisal. Further, great differences in human values seem to have deeper agreements underlying them. Opposed views on capital punishment reflect a shared concern for human life: opposed views on abortion evidence a common concern for human rights. Perhaps people differ less in their fundamental moral intuitions and more in how they translate these into practice.

The debate about intuitionism continues, and the reader must be left to form his own judgement. Meanwhile, I will conclude this section by noting one great virtue of intuitionism as an approach to our present problem: a virtue to be heeded as a warning against dangers inherent in other approaches. We may reflect on the worth of something by asking 'what is the point of it?'. But this way of putting the question can mislead us seriously and even make very worthwhile activities look worthless. For if we question the point of something it sounds as if we want to be shown that it leads on to some further tangible benefit. Thus it is appropriate to ask what is the point of dieting, and to answer that it will improve our health. But if we question the point of music, we may be unable to think of any great benefit it yields, and so conclude that music is worthless. If we question the point of reading poetry, we may end up saying that it extends our vocabulary: which is probably true, but absurdly irrelevant to the worth of poetry as poetry. Again, if we ask about the point of science we are likely to end up stressing the benefits of technology and forgetting science as an exploration of nature. In doing philosophy there is always a danger that by posing questions wrongly we will set ourselves on the wrong track. Intuitionism insists that we focus on the thing itself and not on its by-products.

II Naturalistic Theories of Justification

If we cannot say that the pursuit of some kinds of knowledge is self-evidently a good for man, then perhaps it is possible to deduce what things are good for man from an understanding of man's nature. This promises to be a more objective and scientific approach based on facts rather than questionable intuitions. However, different views of the good for man have been derived from different views of man's nature. Some of these we are about to explore.

For much of human history it has seemed natural to view the universe as embodying a design or purpose, with man as central to that design. The earth's surface with man upon it seemed to be the centre of things; and much in the universe, from the ordered progression of the planets to the efficient purposiveness of plants, animals and men, seemed to be the work of an intelligent designer. Knowing the nature of man was, therefore, a matter of understanding his distinctive place or purpose within the grand design, of discerning that which marked him off from other beings and pointed to his special role in the cosmos. Philosophers call this approach teleological from the Greek word *telos* meaning an end or purpose. But in time it became increasingly difficult to take such a view. Astronomers revealed a universe too large and too old for man to be able to view himself as central, and Darwin's theory of evolution showed how the apparent design in nature *might* be attributed to accident. New ways of understanding man's nature had to be developed, as will be evident in what follows.

Rational Man

Among early philosophers, Aristotle developed the most strikingly teleological view of man. In book I of his *Nicomachean Ethics* he opens his inquiry into the good for man by saying that almost everyone agrees in calling this *eudaemonia*. Unfortunately there is no exact English equivalent to this word. Many translators use 'happiness', but this suggests pleasure: a view of the good life which Aristotle explicitly rejects. Expressions like 'well-being' or 'the good life' may be nearer the mark, though they raise more questions than they answer. *Eudaemonia* is that which is supremely good for man, or good for man as an end in itself and not as a means to some further end. But such a definition strikes Aristotle as platitudinous.

> Some more distinctive account of it is still required. This might perhaps be achieved by grasping what is the function of man. If we take a flautist or a sculptor or any artist – or in general any class of men who have a special function or activity – his goodness and proficiency is considered to lie in the performance of that function; and the same will be true of man, assuming that man has a function. . . . Just as we can see that eye and hand and foot and every one of our members has some function, should we not assume that in like manner a human being has a function over and above these particular functions? (1097b)

This distinctively human function cannot be a function like nutrition or growth which man shares with plants, nor can it be the sentient function shared with other animals. What distinguishes man is that only he is rational. 'The function of man is an activity of the soul in accordance with, or implying, a rational principle' (1098a). Returning to this theme in book X, Aristotle says that if the good life is activity according to virtue then it is reasonable that it should be according to the highest virtue. And the highest virtue for man will be the virtue of man's distinctive function, reason. So the good life is the life of reason or contemplation. Further advantages of this life are that it affords pleasures of great purity and permanence, it can be continuous and it is self-sufficient. Moreover 'contemplation would seem to be the only activity that is appreciated for its own sake; because nothing is gained from it except the act of contemplation, whereas from practical activities we expect to gain something more or less over and above the action' (1177a).

This was a classic teleological argument for the intrinsic worth of knowledge: man being distinguished by his power of reason, the best life for man is the exercise of reason in the pursuit and contemplation of knowledge. Many subsequent thinkers have re-worked this argument. I will consider just two versions, from J. H. Newman's essay *On the Scope and Nature of University Education* (1915 [1852]), and from the educational writings of the eminent modern American philosopher Brand Blanshard.

Newman's discourses on university education were a series of lectures delivered in 1850 when he became rector of the new Catholic university in Dublin. At the time a Catholic university in Britain was a controversial novelty, and Newman was much concerned to set studies there in the right direction, particularly as he thought universities were regaining their old cultural ascendancy as generators of ideas that would shape history. Himself very well educated, Newman understood the variety of ways in which knowledge can have value – equipping us for a profession or citizenship, informing our religious awareness, or enjoyed as an end in itself – the same knowledge often being simultaneously valuable under these different heads. For present purposes discourse IV, 'Liberal knowledge its own end', is important.

Newman says the central concern of a university should be a liberal education, understood as a free education having to do with the mind, by contrast with a servile education, which has to do with bodily labour, mechanical employment, commerce, or a profession. He endorses Aristotle's distinction between what is useful because it 'bears fruit' and what is liberal because it is to be enjoyed though it leads on to nothing else of consequence. The liberal knowledge which should be the proper concern of a university as a good in itself is not *any* kind of knowledge but the systematic knowledge which Newman refers to as 'philosophy' or 'science', making rather unusual use of these terms.

Knowledge is capable of being its own end. Such is the constitution of the human mind, that any kind of knowledge, if it be really such, is its own reward. And if this is true of all knowledge, it is true also of that special Philosophy which I have made to consist in a comprehensive view of truth in all its branches, of the relations of science to science, of their mutual bearings, and their respective values . . . it is an object, in its own nature so really and undeniably good, as to be the compensation of a great deal of thought in the compassing, and a great deal of trouble in the attaining. (Newman, 1915, p. 94)

And later he says of knowledge:

That further advantages accrue to us and redound to others by its possession, over and above what it is in itself, I am very far indeed from denying; but, independent of these, we are satisfying a direct need of our nature in its very acquisition. (ibid., p. 95)

Newman, then, sees knowledge as both good in itself and a source of other goods. While he does not make Aristotle's claim that the pursuit and enjoyment of knowledge is the highest good for man rather than one good among many, his argument is thoroughly Aristotelian. So too is his reason for especially esteeming what he calls 'philosophical' or 'scientific' knowledge:

It seems to me improper to call that passive sensation or perception of things, which brutes seem to possess, by the name of Knowledge. When I speak of Knowledge, I mean something intellectual, something which grasps what it perceives through the senses; something which takes a view of things; which sees more than the senses convey; which reasons upon what it sees and while it sees; which invests it with an idea. (ibid., p. 104)

Blanshard's version of the Aristotelian approach (Blanshard, 1973) is doubly unusual. First, it incorporates a Darwinian view of man which, we noted, is generally taken to be opposed to the teleological view. Secondly, Blanshard supplements the Aristotelian theme with his own view of knowledge. In the tradition of un-Aristotelian thinkers like Spinoza and Hegel, he sees human knowledge as striving towards an ideal of complete rational unity of all truth. Thus he unites two themes to give grounds for valuing knowledge in general and for grading the worth of different kinds of knowledge. First, there is the explicitly Aristotelian view of knowledge as a need of human nature. 'Any theory of education should be natural, in the sense of being based on human nature and the ends that human nature appoints; the education of man is not the same as the training of a parrot, a seal, or a chimpanzee, because human nature has capacities and yearnings denied to other living things' (p. xi). Secondly, there is the denial of Aristotle's view that this cognitive drive is unique to man. Blanshard thinks it is present in all perception and can be found far down the evolutionary chain. But man brings it to a higher level, achieving rational thought which aims to understand all things as parts of an intelligible whole. Accordingly subjects are the more worth studying the more fully they enable us to understand the world we live in. Volcanology and conchology, for example, may interest specialists but in general are of less value than physics and the principles of biology which illumine much larger areas of the world. Ultimately, Blanshard believes, the world can be understood as a series of logical connections, so that the highest form of understanding is the logical: for 'if one has reached it, one has so complete an answer to the question Why? that it cannot intelligibly be raised again?' (p. ix). Aesthetic enjoyment, on the other hand, is thought to be subjective and uninformative, and earns a very low grading.

> Knowledge seems to me to have a very different status among the values of life from that of the other values, such as beauty, comfort and love. Knowledge is at once fulfillment and revelation – fulfillment of the desire to know and revelation of a world outside. The other values lack this revelatory character. The beauty that we find in music, for example, is not a beauty that exists out there apart from our hearing the music, as two planets and two others would still make four apart from our knowing the fact; the

beauty of the music lies solely in the fulfillment and satisfaction realized in the experience of it. (pp. xiii–xiv)

Thus Blanshard makes an important addition to the Aristotelian view, claiming that rational or logical understanding not only meets a distinctively human need, but also gives the fullest possible understanding of how things are. As well as an argument from the nature of man, he has an argument from the nature of knowledge of the kind to be considered in the next section. But it should be noted that one could endorse this double valuation of knowledge without accepting Blanshard's order of grading. As Blanshard is aware, his views go contrary to the climate of contemporary philosophy which is generally unsympathetic to the notion that logic and reasoning can achieve some complete and unified understanding of things. And readers will be familiar with the claims that are often made for other disciplines. Many scientists believe that theirs is the ultimate in knowledge, not because it is rational, but because it is based on observation; while historians and novelists claim to get closer to reality by attending to actual situations in their concrete particularity; and some theorists hold that in aesthetic enjoyment we discover ultimate truths too profound for verbal expression. These points will be raised again, but we must now consider some general objections to the Aristotelian approach.

First, it is far from clear that Aristotle was right to seize on rationality and the desire to know as *the* distinctive features of man. Others have argued that what is really important is the prehensile thumb which enables man to manipulate nature and develop technology; or that what we value most about human beings is their capacity for a range and refinement of emotions apparently denied to other creatures; or that mankind alone appears to be capable of moral choice. We shall shortly be considering other educational theories that emphasise other aspects of human nature.

That it was Greek philosophers who first saw rationality as the supremely important human characteristic nicely underlines the point; the ancient Greeks being noted for having developed reasoning capacities that other cultures have neglected. Perhaps Aristotle was evidencing a cultural bias. Furthermore, the uniqueness of human reason does not guarantee its worth. Many far from frivolous thinkers have seen it as some kind of flaw or corruption (consider, for example, D. H. Lawrence, some Christian mystics, many Zen Buddhists and the 'philosophers' of the Beat Generation).

Notwithstanding such points, the Aristotelian view must be allowed considerable weight: for we could hardly be persuaded by any theory of the worth of knowledge that ignored man's rational and cognitive powers. Blanshard's position gains strength because he supplements a view of man with a view of knowledge: but before we can explore this latter approach, we must consider some other theories of man.

Hedonic Man

Some readers may have felt impatient with the previous section. Such emphasis on rationality suggests a group of intellectuals generalising their own peculiar preferences to include all mankind, many of whom may see no intrinsic value in knowledge and reason. What all people *do* care about is being happy. And this being so, the problem of curriculum justification is not at all difficult in principle: we should teach things which will make people happier. The only problem is the practical one of knowing which things these are.

To argue this is to share the view of a group of eighteenth- and nineteenth-century philosophers known as the English utilitarians (using the word 'utilitarian' in a rather special sense). These philosophers were so impressed by the human desire to avoid pain and secure happiness that they believed all matters of right and wrong should be judged exclusively by reference to what was most likely to bring about the greatest happiness of the greatest number. They did not think that the nature of man reflected some *telos* according to which he ought to live. Rather they sought to solve problems of human life and values scientifically. Science uses observation, and observation tells us that man wants happiness. Facing any decision about, say, a personal moral problem, a political reform, or planning a curriculum, we ought to follow that course of action most likely to increase human pleasure or happiness and least likely to produce pain or unhappiness. Jeremy Bentham, the 'founding father' of the movement, also hoped to follow science by making human goods a matter of careful computation, explaining how we should measure the utility of our actions by weighing the units of pleasure likely to result from our actions (Bentham, 1907, ch. IV).

To avoid misunderstanding, two things must be emphasised about the utilitarian ethic. First, it is not a selfish ethic whereby everyone pursues his own happiness. Rather one is to aim at the maximum happiness of all, sometimes sacrificing personal pleasure for the happiness of others. Secondly, the utilitarian makes pleasure or happiness the only criterion of good. Many philosophers have regarded happiness as *one* good among others such as honesty, freedom, or knowledge; but for the utilitarian such things have no value in their own right and are only good if they help to increase happiness.

The attractions of utilitarianism include its straightforward simplicity and the fact that it can guide all human activities, including education. Indeed, Bentham's friend James Mill worked out a utilitarian theory of education on the principle that the aims of education should be 'To render the individual, as much as possible, an instrument of happiness, first to himself and next to other beings' (Burston, 1969, p. 41), and outlining ways to achieve this. We should note that there are really two educational aims here: to make the pupil happier and to make him likely to bring happiness to others. This duality is echoed by a contemporary utilitarian educationist, Robin Barrow:

> Education should seek to develop children in such a way that they acquire interests, characteristics and competences that enable them both to take pleasure in ways that do not harm others (ideally in ways that contribute to the pleasure of others as well) and also to contribute to the promotion of pleasure and the diminution of pain in general, by the way in which they behave and through the talents they possess. (Barrow, 1976, p. 101)

Our present concern is with the first of these aims. If we educate a pupil so that he will make others happier, then what we teach is valuable instrumentally rather than intrinsically. What we teach a person in order to make *him* happy will include things that are instrumentally good (for example, knowledge to help him earn a living) and things that seem to be cases of intrinsic goods (for example, knowledge of art or astronomy, that is valued regardless of whether it has practical use). On this last point Bentham is splendidly clear: the value of such knowledge is entirely a matter of the happiness it affords. As he puts it, if they give equal pleasure there is absolutely nothing to choose between 'poetry and pushpin'. The inclusion of a subject in the curriculum 'for its own sake' would be justified if the learner was likely to find pleasure in it, now or later.

If accepted, then, the utilitarian doctrine provides an answer to the question with which this book is concerned. However, while few would doubt that human happiness is *a* good, there are difficulties with the utilitarian view that it is the *only* good. Five of these are as follows.

(1) Utilitarians have been notoriously weak on ultimate justification. Thus Bentham said of the pleasure principle:

> Is it susceptible of any direct proof? It should seem not; for that which is used to prove everything else, cannot itself be proved: a chain of proofs must have their commencement somewhere. To give such proofs is as impossible as it is needless. (Bentham, 1907, p. 4)

Few commentators have found this persuasive! And in his essay on utilitarianism James Mill's son John Stuart Mill hardly does any better. Facing the question why happiness is desirable above all else, he says:

> The only proof capable of being given that an object is visible, is that people actually see it. The only proof that a sound is audible, is that people hear it: and so of the other sources of our experience. In like manner, I apprehend, the sole evidence it is possible to produce that anything is desirable, is that people do actually desire it. (Mill, 1910, p. 32)

G. E. Moore commented on this passage:

> Well, the fallacy in this step is so obvious, that it is quite wonderful how Mill failed to see it. The fact is that

'desirable' does not mean 'able to be desired' as 'visible' means 'able to be seen'. The desirable means simply what *ought* to be desired or *deserves* to be desired; . . . Mill has, then, smuggled in, under cover of the word 'desirable', the very notion about which he ought to be quite clear. (Moore, 1960, p. 67)

Of course it may be possible to make a more satisfactory case for utilitarianism, but none such seems to be present in the classic statements.

(2) The utilitarians seem to be mistaken in supposing that a satisfactory theory of value can be based on the happiness criterion alone. Clearly the utilitarians themselves have favoured not just the maximisation of pleasure: they have also wanted to see it distributed as fairly as possible. Whether or not they acknowledge it as Barrow does (Barrow, 1976, p. 89), this involves them in embracing a second principle: that of distributive justice. Furthermore, utilitarians do not just adopt their principle arbitrarily, but because they think it is true: thus they value truth as well as happiness and justice.

(3) This and the next two points raise doubts about the utilitarian notion of pleasure as something that can be isolated, quantified and pursued as an aim. In a lively attack, Karl Marx complains about Bentham's parochial view of man. He first insults Bentham as 'the arch philistine . . . the insipid, pedantic, leather tongued oracle of the commonplace bourgeois intelligence'. Then he makes the serious point:

He that would pass judgment upon all human activities, movements, relations, etc., in accordance with the principle of utility, must first become acquainted with human nature in general, and then with human nature as modified in each specific historical epoch. But Bentham makes short work of it. In his arid and simple way, he assumes the modern petty bourgeois, and above all the modern English petty bourgeois, to be the normal man. Whatever seems useful to this queer sort of normal man and to his world, is regarded as useful in and by itself. By this yardstick, Bentham proceeds to measure everything past, present, and to come. (Marx, 1930, p. 671)

This has been echoed by a modern Marxist. In a discussion of educational aims, MacIntyre (1964) contends that whatever its proponents may have intended, in actuality utilitarianism will always be interpreted in terms of the beliefs and attitudes dominant in society so that where utilitarianism reigns people will be encouraged to seek satisfactions in the prevailing pleasures of that society. (In our society he identifies these as the pleasures of acquisitive materialism.) The point is that utilitarianism seeks a scientific knowledge of the good for man by observing man, observing both that people like happiness and what things give people happiness. This is bound to involve a restricted vision: for a view of the good for man based on observation of the satisfaction people *actually* find can only attend to the satisfactions people have learned to enjoy in a particular society: the utilitarian blocks himself off from exploring hitherto unknown rewards in new life-styles.

(4) The last point might not trouble a strict Benthamite who could say that it is the maximisation of pleasure that matters, not the exploration of new and perhaps richer satisfactions. However, one utilitarian, John Stuart Mill, did concern himself with a related point. Sensitive to the range and variety of human pleasures, Mill was convinced that some pleasures were superior in quality to others, that the difference between the pleasures of poetry and pushpin was not just quantitative. He agreed with those who 'assign to the pleasures of the intellect, of the feelings and imagination, and of the moral sentiments, a much higher value as pleasures than to those of mere sensation'. It is, he says

> quite compatible with the principle of utility to recognise the fact, that some *kinds* of pleasure are more desirable and more valuable than others. It would be absurd that while, in estimating all other things, quality is considered as well as quantity, the estimation of pleasures should be supposed to depend on quality alone. (Mill, 1910, p. 7)

These qualitatively superior pleasures are recognisable as such because 'of two pleasures, if there be one to which all or almost all who have experience of both give a decided preference, irrespective of any feeling of moral obligation to prefer it, that is the more desirable pleasure' (p. 8).

Now many will agree that some pleasures are qualitatively superior to others, and that this is evident to those who have adequately experienced both sorts. But Mill is generally thought to have made a rather serious and obvious mistake in contending that he could hold this and still call himself a utilitarian. For the original utilitarian position is quite clear: it is quantity of pleasure, and quantity of pleasure alone, that matters. To distinguish between two pleasures in terms of quality is to introduce some further standard: to evaluate pleasure in terms of something other than pleasure. One who does this is no longer a utilitarian.

But perhaps there is more than a confusion involved here. Why did a fine thinker like Mill make such an obvious mistake? Could he have been vaguely aware of something seriously wrong with the utilitarian view of pleasure?

(5) Certainly some philosophers have believed there is something wrong here, and doubted whether it is true that people desire pleasure or happiness as such. Is it not the case that we learn to desire things, and that in achieving these we find pleasure? I do not listen to music because I want to become happy: rather, I want to listen to music, and when I am able to do this I become happy. Surely this is why thoughtful educators encounter the problems with which this book is concerned. Their problem is not whether to teach children about sources of pleasure: it is to decide which things to teach children to value so that they may become sources of pleasure.

This conclusion is strengthened if we follow Moore's advice and carefully focus our attention on the subject of evaluation. A popular philosophical 'thought experiment' will help. Suppose we reflect on some things that give us great pleasure (say, a favourite game, enjoying an art work, love-making, or studying an interesting subject) and then ask ourselves: if some quite harmless drug could give me the pleasure afforded by my chosen activity without my having actually to engage in it, then would I forsake the activity for the drug? Some may answer 'Yes' or 'No' to this hypothetical question, but the point of the exercise is that many will doubt whether it makes sense to talk of having the pleasure of an activity apart from engaging in it.

But in that case it seems to be the activity that matters, not the pleasure: and there is something wrong with a philosophy of value that talks abstractly of the maximisation of pleasure.

Problem-Solving Man

John Dewey, the most influential modern educational philosopher, proposed no theory to help us recognise what knowledge is of greatest intrinsic worth, for he believed that no knowledge can have such worth. But he did not therefore preclude the possibility of distinguishing what is and is not of educational worth. Rather his notions of growth and experience give him a basis for choosing a curriculum while denying any final ends or values for man. The reasons for this lie partly in his democratic commitment and partly in the influence of Darwinism on his view of man. He sees the traditional idea of a liberal education as anti-democratic because it involves the pursuit of knowledge for its own sake by a privileged and leisured few, while everyone else learns to do productive or useful work.

According to Darwinian theory, mankind and other species evolved accidentally in the struggle of creatures to survive. Thus man developed his intelligence as a 'tool' or 'organ' to help grapple with the environment, just as other creatures evolved claws, wings, fangs, trunks, and so on. Intelligence helps us to avoid predators, to protect ourselves from the weather and to feed ourselves. In a word, intelligence is useful, and there is no reason to think of the human mind as equipped to achieve knowledge of ultimate and perennial truths. This Darwinian theme was one source of the pragmatic theory of truth associated with C. S. Peirce and William James as well as with Dewey. According to this theory it is a mistake to think of truth as a final revelation of the way things are in reality. Rather to say that a proposition is true is equivalent to saying that it is, at least for the time being, useful in the sense that if we believe it we will be more successful in solving problems in the process of living in the world.

This, of course, is a very simple formulation and though the exponents of the theory did often put it thus they also gave more sophisticated accounts. However, the simple statement is adequate for us to see why Dewey could not believe in objective bodies of knowledge existing and having worth independently of man's practical concerns. For he sees all human knowledge and values as originating in practical experience and problem-solving. But he does not therefore advocate a narrowly useful curriculum, or suggest that pupils should determine their own curriculum on the grounds that the value in the learning experiences is the value that pupils themselves find in them. In 1938 he published *Experience and Education* to correct such misunderstandings of a lifetime's work. Experience means not just what happens to someone, but also his conscious understanding of, and response to, whatever he encounters. Traditional schooling often failed to provide for this active element in learning: but it is not enough, as many progressivists believed, just to make the learning experience active. 'Everything depends upon the *quality* of the experience which is had. The quality of any experience has two aspects. There is an immediate aspect of agreeableness or disagreeableness, and there is its influence upon later experiences' (Dewey, 1963, p. 27). The educator should use his mature knowledge and understanding to recognise young learners' initiatives and guide them into experiences that will be found rewarding now and that are likely to lead on to further rewarding experiences. 'Hence the central problem of an education based upon experience is to select the kind of present experiences that live fruitfully and creatively in subsequent experiences' (ibid., pp. 27–8). To critics who doubted whether this was adequate to guide the teacher's selection of experience he replied:

The objection made is that growth might take many different directions: a man, for example, who starts out on a career of burglary may grow in that direction, and by practice may grow into a highly expert burglar. Hence it is argued that 'growth' is not enough; we must also specify the direction in which growth takes place, the end towards which it tends. Before, however, we decide that the objection is conclusive we must analyze the case a little further.

That a man may grow in efficiency as a burglar, as a gangster, or as a corrupt politician, cannot be doubted. But from the standpoint of growth as education and education as growth the question is whether growth in this direction promotes or retards growth in general. Does this form of growth create conditions for further growth, or does it set up conditions that shut off the person who has grown in this particular direction from the occasions, stimuli and opportunities for continuing growth in new directions? What is the effect of growth in a special direction upon the attitudes and habits which alone open up avenues for development in other lines? . . . *only* when development in a particular line conduces to continuing growth does it answer to the criterion of education as growing. (ibid., p. 36)

Dewey does not, of course, believe that the only, or even major, objection to crime and corruption is the harm done to the criminal. His is a democratic and co-operative ethic whereby any action must be judged for its effect on others. Allowing this, however, his position still seems inadequate. Certainly it is important to consider the effect of any activity on the learner's capacity for further satisfying experiences. Dewey could have amplified the point by noting how criminals must blind themselves to the unhappiness they cause, developing a callousness that will make it difficult to enjoy personal affections or social involvement. But it is hard to see how we could go very far with this approach and not encounter the need to make qualitative judgements. For there are sensitivities and possibilities for rewarding experiences that are available to criminal minds and not to morally sensitive citizens. Sooner or later the educator will have to ask: why open up avenues to one kind of experience and not to another?

Imaginative Man

Most educators allow the importance of the imagination: yet there have been no systematic attempts to get to grips with this difficult topic and to understand the place of imagination in human life and education. The one exception is in the work of Mary Warnock who has several times written on the matter (Warnock, 1973, 1976, 1977, 1978), contending that imagination is so important to our nature as human beings that 'we ought to value it and respect it more highly than anything else; and that therefore, if it can be educated and improved, it is to this education that we should give priority' (1978, p. 44).

Before considering Warnock's views, we should note something of the scope and nature of philosophical problems about the imagination. Initially there is what seems to be a merely lexical problem. Brief reflection will bring to mind the diversity of usages we give to the word 'imagination' and cognates like 'image', 'imagine', 'imaginary' and 'imaginative'. Such usages cover the forming of mental images, the creation of works of art, dreaming, fantasising and innovating. And there are evaluative usages for originality of invention and convincingness of imitation. Such diversity may suggest that the use of cognate terms is coincidental, with nothing to be gained by looking for connecting links. Yet we may wonder if our ancestors would have developed such uses had they not sensed some unifying links which we might now elucidate. When we try to do this, however, more than verbal issues are seen to be involved: understanding imagination involves questions about the nature of art, science and, above all, knowledge and the mind. It becomes clear that the imagination is fundamental to the whole nature and working of the human mind.

Two ways of putting 'order' into the notion of imagination must be rejected. The first, once popular with philosophers and psychologists, is to hypothesise a *faculty* of imagination, some hidden power or 'mental muscle' exercised in various activities of mind. The objection to this is that it postulates an entity that may not exist and that we can never know about. Talk of a faculty hides the problem rather than solving it. A second approach suggests that all the diverse exercises of imagination involve or are preceded by the entertaining of mental images. The most important objection to this is that it just does not fit the facts. Many people can imagine or be imaginative without entertaining mental images, and some people do not experience mental images at all.

However, P. F. Strawson (1974) has suggested a refined version of this approach which Warnock follows. Rejecting the idea that all exercises of imagination involve or are preceded by the entertaining of mental images, one can still reflect on what sort of things are involved in being able to entertain a mental image and then look for links between these and other exercises of imagination. In her book Warnock uses a historical approach to track down such links, studying the works of that small number of philosophers and others who have systematically considered the subject. In this way she discovers that the human capacity to entertain images is importantly linked not just to the other activities of the imagination but also to the whole working of the mind. When we form a mental image we reproduce previous sights and sounds, perhaps rearranging them, but knowingly making 'present' to ourselves things that are not present. David Hume, she records, showed that imagination enables us to use language: for when, say, we apply the word dog to one particular dog, we somehow have to have potentially present to our mind a host of different dogs. Further, he showed, imagination is linked to feeling as when an artist moves us by the power of the images he creates. Kant saw that imagination is fundamental to perception, for we are only able to put order into our present perceptions by linking them to retained previous perceptions. The Romantic poets showed how imagination links present perceptions to past perceptions and images so as to fill them with significance, and intimations of greater significance yet to be revealed. Wittgenstein showed connections between imagining and our ability to see the same things in different ways. Sartre showed why works of art are works of imagination; for when we look at a painting we must not see the paint as paint; we must imagine or 'see' it as a landscape, a person, or whatever. And, most important, Sartre represents imagination as the basis of human choice and freedom: for were we not able to image or imagine things as other than they actually are, there would be no possibility of choosing to act, of choosing to change things.

In the end a crisp theory of imagination does not seem to emerge from Warnock's treatment, but this is hardly to be expected of the first thorough-going attempt to sort out such a complex and difficult theme. Certainly she does show us the justification for

> using the name 'imagination' for a collection of human capacities and abilities which seem to cluster together, but which need not, of course, be thought to constitute a

faculty or power totally separate from others in the human range. Elements in this collection are perceptual, classificatory, linguistic . . . and emotional. Mental imagery, memory, insight and understanding are all linked in the collection. (Warnock, 1978, p. 45)

A view of the imagination as so powerful, pervasive and important naturally suggests that it should also be a central concern of education. In chapter IV of *Schools of Thought* (1977) Warnock proposes three ingredients of the good life which are therefore also the three proper aims of education. Two of these, virtue and work, are outside our present concern, and the third is the cultivation of the imagination. It may be, however, that she is able to make such strong claims for the imagination because she has defined it so broadly as to include the whole functioning of the human mind. An unusually long quotation seems appropriate here:

I use the term to cover a human capacity shared by everyone who can perceive and think, who can notice things and can experience emotions (that is by virtually everyone who is subject to education . . .) Imagination in this sense is involved in all perception of the world, in that it is that element in perception which makes what we see and hear meaningful to us. It is the element, that is, by means of which we characterize and feel things to be familiar, unfamiliar, beautiful, desirable, strange, horrible, and so on. Being the image-making capacity, it is also involved in memory of the past and the envisaging of the future, as well as in that kind of dreaming and day dreaming which is neither memory nor prediction, but fantasy. Its connexion, therefore, with creativity, and especially with artistic creation, is central; but its exercise is by no means confined to this. Those who perceive, dream or remember with heightened imagination may, often do, long to express in some form what it is that they perceive, but they may not necessarily even try to do so. However, the creative character of imagination is manifest, even if nothing is 'made' except the significance or meaning to the observer of the world he perceives. In that everybody inhabits a world which has some meaning, everyone possesses imagination. And this is proved, even if the meanings are perfectly ordinary, for instance, that this is an object which could be used as a tool; that this is a table which has always stood in the same place. But deeper reflection, noticing more, thinking about things more consistently, feeling about them more strongly, these are all things we can learn to do, and all of them increase the world we live in. (Warnock, 1977, pp. 151–2)

The key point seems to lie in the last sentence: Warnock thinks imagination is most powerfully and significantly at work when we perceive things with feeling in a rich, lively way, aware of the possibility of enriching our perceptions further, learning more about them and making the world more significant for us. It is the cultivation of such rich and heightened perceptions that she has in mind in advocating the cultivation of imagination as a major educational aim. The value of this, she says, does not need to be argued, for 'while everyone exercises imagination in some degree, the desirability of exercising it more is not to be defended on the grounds that it leads to anything good, though it may well do so, but simply on the grounds that, if understood, it will be seen to *be* good!' (ibid., p. 153).

We may well find this last move unsatisfactory: and we must also note in passing that what Warnock understands by the education of the imagination is not what is meant by many educationists who would make creativity and invention central. A thorough critique of Warnock's theory would have to consider whether her emphasis does indeed follow from an adequate understanding of the imagination. For the present, however, we must attend to the educational implications she draws:

> If a particular study can be shown to increase the imaginative powers of a child, then it is a strong candidate for inclusion in the educational curriculum, granted that the point of that curriculum is to offer to the child the possibility of a better life than he could have had without it. So it is necessary next to consider what kinds of studies can be described as imagination-enhancing. (loc. cit.)

Having said this, Warnock does not try to appraise the worth of various subject matters as imagination-enhancers: for what she thinks is important to this end is not so much the actual subject matter but that there be considerable pupil specialisation and choice. Specialisation is important because the enhanced and informed perception in which she is interested requires a lot of work to achieve a rich understanding of any one subject matter. While breadth of knowledge is desirable, if the range of subjects taught is too great 'it is simply impossible for the student's imagination to be fired in such a way that he can go on from what he has been taught to what he wants to think of or do for himself. And the purpose of all education is to seek this freedom to go on' (Warnock, 1973, p. 120). Nor can teachers of a broad curriculum be expected to exhibit the mastery and enthusiasm necessary to excite their pupils.

Pupil choice is important because, as the Romantics showed, there is something very personal about the imaginative vision, so that different pupils will respond differently to different subjects. The extent and timing of such choice is not specified though Warnock certainly does not intend the openness of the free-schooler, for she describes school as 'a kind of institutionalised stimulus, to prevent the sudden and sporadic removal of the motive to go on, such as is familiar among children left to themselves' (Warnock, 1977, p. 153). 'The teacher', she says 'will be in a position to direct the attention of his pupils to things which they would not otherwise see, hear or read' (ibid., p. 161).

If we now ask whether Warnock's vision of the cultivation of the imagination as an educational aim provides us with a satisfactory basis for curriculum selection, then it would seem not, for several reasons. In the first place, her theory of the imagination may risk being too broad to be informative. She argues that the imagination is important to every function of mind. But to say then that education should be concerned with the development of imagination seems to be the same as to say that it should be concerned with the development of mind: with the emphasis on keeping the mind lively and excited rather than developing it in any specific direction or towards any vision of completeness. As Warnock herself says, 'the imagination, in the sense in which I have been talking about it, is identical with the capacity for free thought' (Warnock, 1973, p. 121).

In other respects there seems to be an incompleteness in her account of the imagination which is reflected in the educational conclusions. Many theorists have seen the imagination as the image-making power, and so as related to the mind's power to think in concrete particulars: thus imagination can be contrasted with reason or the capacity to think in abstract and general terms. And presumably it is desirable that the curriculum help us learn to think well both with generalities and with particulars, to develop our reason as well as our imagination.

At the same time, there is an important sense in which the imagination *is* a rational faculty: a faculty that can and does operate under the governance of reason, knowledge and understanding. (We sometimes express this point by contrasting the imagination with fantasy.) But if the working of imagination can be informed by knowledge, then surely in designing a curriculum to cultivate the imagination we cannot by-pass questions about what knowledge should be selected to inform the developing imagination. Warnock says that 'to exercise the imagination is to keep it in practice, by giving it to attend to, in detail, objects which are worthy of attention; and all objects are more worthy of attention in detail than superficially' (loc. cit.). Is it not surprising that she should say this without facing the need to judge what objects are worth attending to, whether in detail or superficially? Certainly there can be little intrinsic value in studying things about which one does not become excited: but it does not follow that nothing else is relevant to deciding what is worth knowing about. There seems to be justice in a comment of R. S. Peters, that 'Mary Warnock views subjects rather from the point of view of potential research workers; but an equally important educational question is to ask how the products of such work can become significant to the majority of people who are never going to transform such products by their own activity' (Peters, 1977a, p. 55). As far as the typical learner is concerned, Warnock seems to by-pass rather than resolve the question of what knowledge is most worthy of study.

Man as a Striver

It might be thought that particularly strong arguments are needed to show the intrinsic value of learned and cultural pursuits because they can cost so much in terms of human stress and suffering. Scholars and researchers often pursue knowledge so single-mindedly as to bring on exhaustion, loneliness and illness. That an activity can put such strains on a person sounds like an argument for not pursuing it. Yet it can be held that this element of striving against difficulty and adversity is at least part of what gives value to many human enterprises, including the pursuit of knowledge. This view may seem less paradoxical if we reflect that we admire those who strive valiantly against great odds, even if they fail or if we disapprove of the objects of their striving. And most of us are drawn to some activities not despite but because of the fact that they promise more striving than pleasure. One may choose to go on a tough mountain walk knowing that delight in the air and scenery will not outweigh aching limbs and sore feet.

That such striving affords value to human life was argued in the eighteenth century by Immanuel Kant who rejected fashionable hopes that progress in knowledge would increase man's control over nature and human affairs to usher in an age of maximum human happiness. Hostile nature and man's own destructive tendencies were such, he thought, that there could be no end to human misery. In section 83 of his *Critique of Judgement* he says:

> Nature has not taken him [man] for her special darling and favoured him with benefit above all animals. Rather, in her destructive operations, – plague, hunger, perils of waters, frost, assaults of other animals great and small, etc., – in these things has she spared him as little as any other animal. Further, the inconsistency of his own *natural dispositions* drives him into self-devised torments, and also reduces others of his own race to misery, by the oppression of lordship, the barbarism of war, and so forth. (Kant, 1914, pp. 353–4)

And man's pursuit of happiness is further bound to be frustrated: for as he fulfils one desire he thereby becomes a

34

changed person with new desires. 'It is not his nature to rest and be contented with the possession and enjoyment of anything whatever' (ibid., p. 353). So we cannot believe that the value of human life consists in happiness. We should instead seek the value of human life not in what happens to man, but in what he does. Man is not just a part of nature, a creature of appetites and inclinations: he is also a rational being capable of freely choosing to do what reason says he ought to do rather than what inclination wants to do. Virtue consists in struggling to overcome the inclinations of nature in order to follow reason.

So culture and civilisation are valuable not as sources of comfort and mental delights, but because they provide the demanding norms and standards whereby man can test and prove his ability to rise above natural inclinations. 'Hostile' nature too makes her contribution by challenging us to overcome adversity:

> Without it all excellent tendencies in mankind would forever lie dormant and undeveloped. Man desires concord, but nature knows better what is good for his species: nature desires discord. Man wants to live in ease and comfort; but nature aims to shake him out of his lethargy and passive satisfaction into toil and labour. (Quoted in Cassirer, 1945a, p. 41)

On such a view the great disciplines of learning would have value because they require us to strive to master and add to the store of human knowledge. Like nature, scholarship can shake man out of lethargy into toil and labour.

Similar themes are developed by a modern philosopher, R. K. Elliott (1977). Elliott criticises R. S. Peters (whose views are considered later) for attending to the human values of pleasure and rationality, but neglecting 'vitality'. People admire and value the stretching of our powers to the utmost, even when this is not necessary; and demanding scholarship gives scope for such living at the height of our powers. A life full of such striving would not be a life wasted even if it were a life without great pleasure. But, Elliott allows, such expenditure of power would seem absurd were it not in the pursuit of knowledge worth having: knowledge that matters to us as human beings. So while we can find value in a life of striving for knowledge and understanding, this requires us to know what knowledge is worth striving for. A recognition of the values man can find in striving does not answer our question: it brings us back to it by requiring that such striving have a worthy point.

Naturalistic Theories: Conclusion

Considering a number of theories which draw conclusions about the good life and education for man from views of man's nature, we have found important insights in all these theories. Yet each approach was found wanting. Indeed, this might have been anticipated: for while there could hardly be a theory of education without a theory of human nature, there are reasons why a theory of human nature on its own is unlikely to be adequate to tell us what educators ought to do.

First, there are difficulties in giving an account of human nature that does justice to its subject matter. One of these is suggested by the discussion so far: for each of the theories considered seizes on one aspect of man and offers it either as a whole account of man or as an account of what is most important about man. Confronting the complexity of man's nature, theorists are tempted to focus on one aspect and to neglect others. And as well as complexity, there is the problem of variability. Studies such as history and anthropology show us how greatly people's lives have varied between ages and cultures – varied in much more than adaptation to physical circumstances. With different beliefs about themselves, the world and the divine, people behave very differently and respond to different desires, ambitions and ideals. Sometimes we learn of people in cultures so different from our own that we are puzzled to understand how they could think and live as they do. We can reduce the puzzle only by learning more about their way of seeing the world. In doing this we see how human nature can take on forms very different from what is familiar in the culture we happen to inhabit. Indeed, some theorists are so impressed by this human variability that they say there is no such thing as *a* human nature.

Other theorists think such views are overstated and contend

that underlying all the variations between people are important common characteristics. But the problem is to say what these common traits are. If we attend to what is most obviously common to all human beings, then we risk describing human nature in terms of things such as biological needs and basic appetites which we share with other animals and which clearly are not distinctively human. But attempts to focus on what *is* distinctively human take us into the realm of the vague and controversial. It is understandable if regrettable that speculation about human nature often derives as much from studies of other animals as from studies of men. But such speculations just cannot take sufficient account of how we become very different people by being differently educated.

A further problem is that even if we do achieve a satisfactory account of human nature it remains doubtful whether we can draw conclusions about how men *ought* to be educated from facts about what *is* the nature of man. G. E. Moore coined the expression 'naturalistic fallacy' (Moore, 1960, p. 10) to describe any ethical reasoning that confused 'is' and 'ought' questions, as happens when we use assertions about what *is* the case to justify conclusions about what ought to be. Statements about what men are like are factual statements, while statements about how men ought to be educated express value judgements. It seems to be a mistake to think we can derive the latter from the former.

This is not to say that facts about human nature have no relevance to practical educational decisions. How could they? Indeed, some philosophers doubt whether the is/ought distinction is as clear as Moore and others maintain. Perhaps the naturalistic fallacy is not always a fallacy. However, the point remains that to state the nature of man cannot, *on its own*, be enough to justify a curriculum. Something further must be said regarding why some kinds of knowledge and not others are appropriate to that nature, and why that nature should be developed in one direction rather than another. Clearly we need to consider other possible bases on which to construct a theory of educational worth.

III Answers from the Nature of Knowledge

This section considers three thinkers according to whom it is in terms of the nature of knowledge that the worth of knowledge is to be assessed. We have already encountered this idea in Blanshard's view of liberal education. Here we attend to a classical philosopher, Plato, who graded different kinds of knowledge into a hierarchy, and to two contemporary philosophers whose views, while differing in important respects, are close enough for them to have collaborated on one book. Peters and Hirst argue the importance of educating children into all the disciplines or forms of knowledge without setting one above the other: Hirst attending to the mapping out of various forms of knowledge and Peters to the problem of justification.

Plato

One approach to Plato's view of knowledge is by way of the famous metaphor of the cave which introduces his plans to educate that small elite destined to become philosopher-kings in his ideal state. In book VII of *The Republic* he says:

> Picture the enlightenment or ignorance of our human conditions somewhat as follows. Imagine an underground chamber, like a cave with an entrance open to the daylight and running a long way underground. In this chamber are men who have been prisoners there since they were children, their legs and necks being so fastened that they can only look straight ahead of them and cannot turn their heads. Behind them and above them a fire is burning, and between the fire and the prisoners runs a road, in front of which a curtain-wall has been built, like the screen at puppet shows between the operators and their audience above which they show their puppets . . . Imagine further that there are men carrying all sorts of gear along behind the curtain-wall, including figures of men and animals made of wood and stone and other materials, and that some of these men, as is natural, are talking and some not.
> (pp. 514–15)

Unable to see anything for themselves, of their fellows, or the traffic on the road, these prisoners will assume that the shadows on the back of the cave are the real thing. If they are freed to turn towards the light and the travellers on the road, they will be dazzled and perplexed by it all and want to return to the shadows. They will only be totally freed if someone drags them into the light until they get accustomed to looking at actual people. Only then will the former prisoners learn to despise their original condition.

The point of the metaphor is twofold. First, the condition of the bound prisoners represents the actual state of most of us living in the world of sensory perception and taking it that what we see, feel, taste, hear and smell is real and true. We make this mistake because we have known nothing better. Secondly, the process of escaping or being dragged from the shadows is the process of being educated into a truer understanding than comes from mere sense perception. For the world of sensory perception is itself only a world of shadow or illusion: a pale, unreliable reflection of the true world that we can only come to know by way of a demanding education of our rational rather than our sensory powers. Such an education is valuable because it brings us to real knowledge instead of what is widely taken for knowledge.

Plato knew he was saying something *prima facie* very odd. Common sense suggests that knowledge based on the testimony of the senses is the most 'solid' and dependable there is. Yet Plato proposes to liberate us from this sensible world into a world of abstract ideas which, he says, are more real and knowable than the objects of sensory perception. How could such improbable suggestions have seemed reasonable? One consideration that weighed with Plato was that the testimonies of our senses are notoriously inconsistent: the same thing can appear very differently to different people, or to the same person looking at it from a different angle, in a different light, or after a drink. Furthermore, knowledge is of the truth and the truth is surely true for ever, while the things in the world of our senses are endlessly changing. So if we are to be able to know anything, then there must be some things to know that are neither ambiguous nor ever-changing as are the objects of our sensory perceptions. Plato believed that there were such things:

that the houses, dogs, trees and triangles that we encounter through our senses are inferior copies of the forms or ideas of houses, dogs, trees and triangles. These forms of things are unambiguous and everlasting. We cannot perceive them through our senses but we can know them by our powers of rational understanding: and to come to know them really is to achieve knowledge. We may better understand this theory of the forms if we trace through two of the considerations that led Plato to develop it.

(1) Plato's teacher Socrates encouraged discussion of moral issues; and people talking seriously about things like honesty, justice and virtue will feel a need to define their terms precisely. Socrates believed there were such things as *real* courage, *real* honesty and *real* virtue: and that we needed to know them. Plato extended this interest to knowledge and definitions in general. He was struck by the fact that we can apply one particular word such as 'red', 'man', 'virtuous', or 'equal' to a number of different things or situations. From this he concluded something that most modern philosophers deny: that for one word 'red' to have application to a variety of objects there must be some essence of redness to which all these objects approximate. Likewise of other words: there must be some perfect and perennial 'forms' or 'ideas' of redness, manness, virtue and equality on account of which things can be called 'red', 'men', 'virtuous', or 'equal'.

(2) Another of Plato's reasons can be understood by reflecting on what happens when we learn to do geometry. We begin by using words like 'round', 'square' and 'straight' as applied to physical objects like oranges, tables and sticks. Later we draw and measure diagrams not of oranges, tables and sticks but of circles, squares and lines. In time we make a huge jump in our thinking but make it so easily that it probably goes unnoticed. We cease to think just of the triangle we have drawn on the page and start thinking of triangles in general. And along with this goes a more remarkable change. Though we still use our drawn triangles as visual aids we soon learn to talk about triangles that no one ever could draw: for we learn theorems about triangles encompassed by perfectly straight lines with length but no breadth: triangles with internal angles which add up to *precisely* 180 degrees. If we measured our drawn triangles the total would

only be approximately 180 degrees: we learn to show that in a triangle that is thought but not seen the total *must* be *exactly* 180 degrees. And it seems quite natural to describe these invisible figures as 'true', 'perfect', or 'real': to contrast them with the imperfect figures that we draw on paper. Thus geometry leads us away from the imperfect world of the senses to the true world of ideas.

The perfect triangles and circles we have learned to reason about are what Plato called the 'forms' or 'ideas' of triangles and circles. He saw the fact that we can theorise and know about them as grounds for believing that they existed: though, of course, we would miss the point if we asked him to show us one. Himself an able mathematician, he extended this way of thinking to all kinds of knowledge. It seemed to him that just as we can recognise an imperfect drawn circle by referring it to the idea or form of a true circle, similarly we would be unable to appraise persons and things as more or less honest, virtuous, or beautiful, unless we measured them against some idea or 'form' of honesty, virtue, or beauty. Similarly we would be unable to recognise the diversity of trees, chairs and men *as* trees, chairs and men unless we related all the particular instances to the 'form' of a tree, chair, or man. These 'forms' can be known by man not, of course, through his senses but through his reason or intellect. They belong not to the sensible world but to the intelligible world of real knowledge.

We cannot here go into Plato's other reasons for embracing the theory of forms, or his answers to criticisms. Rather we must consider how, from this view of knowledge, he works out a curriculum for the education of philosopher-kings. The details need not detain us: what is important is that after a period of training character, emotion, body and senses the student is to embark on a long course of study, leading his mind from the sensible world of mere opinions to the intelligible world of knowledge. He will begin with natural sciences. These depend on observations in the sensible world, but the emphasis will be on more abstract and mathematical sciences such as astronomy. Progressing to pure mathematics, the student will come closer to knowledge and the forms, though this will not be a complete 'escape' since he will rely upon diagrams in the sensible world. Now, however, he can move into the realm of pure philosophy or reasoning and enjoy that real knowledge which reason apprehends directly by the power of pure thought, so that all dependence on sense is left behind. This is to arrive at real knowledge: it is to complete an education.

Plato's reasons for valuing such an education include the practical point that by coming to know the form of the good the philosopher-kings will acquire a moral expertise, equipping them to rule the republic guided by a certain and dependable knowledge of what is right. But he also values it because it will take the learner away from illusion, ambiguity and opinion to truth: because it is an education in knowledge.

Many readers will find all this unpersuasive. However skilfully Plato argues, it is hard to accept the view that our only real knowledge is of ideas and not of things. Nor do we like to have our most treasured disciplines so decisively down-graded. Indeed, one of many reasons why we ought to take Plato very seriously is precisely that he puts us on our intellectual mettle by mustering powerful arguments that require us to reassess our most profound convictions. However, few modern philosophers believe that there is only one kind of knowledge and that this is indeed knowledge because it puts us in touch with what is perennial, real and true. So it will be appropriate now to contrast Plato with a present day theorist, P. H. Hirst, who also proposes a curriculum derived from a view of knowledge: but a different view of knowledge and a different curriculum.

P. H. Hirst

Hirst's influential view of the curriculum was first outlined in 1965 in his paper 'Liberal education and the nature of knowledge': this has been subsequently included in a collection of his writings on curriculum (Hirst, 1974) to which it will be more convenient to refer. Hirst contends that the term 'liberal education' has been so variously used as to threaten its meaning. Yet it *can* preserve a positive meaning suitable to serious educational planning since it is 'the appropriate label for a positive concept, that of an education based fairly and squarely on the nature of knowledge itself' (Hirst, 1974, p. 30). This notion was developed by the Greeks out of two related philosophical doctrines. First, there was a doctrine about man of the kind we have already encountered in Aristotle: 'that it is the peculiar and distinctive activity of the mind, because of its very nature, to pursue knowledge. The achievement of knowledge satisfies and fulfils the mind which thereby attains its own appropriate end'. And furthermore the pursuit of knowledge is 'the chief means whereby the good life as a whole is to be found' (loc. cit.). Secondly, there were doctrines about knowledge, such as those we have considered in Plato, according to which the mind can use reason to come to know the essential nature of things, can escape from deceptive appearances and doubtful opinions in order to achieve knowledge of what is ultimately real. And, as we have also seen, this notion went along with the view that there is a structured hierarchy in man's understanding.

These doctrines combined to yield a clearly defined and justified idea of liberal education as being simply concerned with the pursuit of knowledge.

> The definition is clear, because education is determined objectively in range, in structure and in content by the forms of knowledge itself and their harmonious, hierarchical inter-relations. There is here no thought of defining education in terms of knowledge and skills that may be useful, or in terms of moral virtues or qualities of mind that may be considered desirable. The definition is stated strictly in terms of man's knowledge of what is the case. The development of the mind to which it leads, be it in skills, virtues or other character-istics, is thought to be necessarily its greatest good. (ibid., p. 31)

The justification is threefold. It is an education based on what is true rather than uncertain opinions and temporary values. Knowledge being a distinctively human value it is an education that fulfils the human mind. And it affords the knowledge essential for man to understand how he ought to live.

So this idea of liberal education is not to be dismissed as no more than an education fit for free men and not for slaves. It is an idea with a perennial appeal, though this is strongest at times when the supportive doctrines flourish: when it is believed that 'knowledge is achieved when the mind attains its own satisfac-tion or good by corresponding to objective reality' (ibid., p. 33). However, it has become increasingly difficult to accept such doctrines; difficult to view knowledge as a matter of the mind coming in a straightforward way to mirror reality. For some philosophers have been struck by the ways in which the nature of the human mind and sense-organs shapes the way we experience the world. Others have noted how fundamentally our view of things is informed and shaped by socially inherited ideas and language, so that people in different cultures learn to see and understand things differently. So it no longer seems tenable to talk with Plato of knowledge directly reflecting or corresponding to the world as it actually is. Rather we experience the world only as it is 'filtered' or 'transformed' through the ways we learn to understand things. Accordingly 'knowledge is no longer seen as the understanding of reality but merely as the understanding of experience' (loc. cit.), and we can no longer justify an education defined in terms of knowledge understood to be a straightforward mirroring of reality.

Hirst thinks this is why some recent thinkers have talked of liberal education in terms not of knowledge, but of the development of abilities and qualities of mind like creativity, effective thinking and judgement. But they put the cart before the horse, for it does not mean very much to talk of developing powers of effective thinking, etc., without first stating the areas of knowledge and understanding in which these powers are to be exercised. Effective thinking in appreciating art works is very different from effective thinking in solving mathematical problems or in deciding how to vote.

This point introduces Hirst's important notion that there are a limited number of distinct and equally valid forms of knowledge (not to be confused with Plato's 'forms'), and that a liberal education gives an understanding of all of them. This view, he says, both accords with modern theories of knowledge and preserves the original Greek notion of an education determined exclusively by the nature of knowledge: though it is now a different education because our view of knowledge has changed. He argues that there are distinct forms of knowledge because the way we experience things is determined by the language through which we understand the world and it is possible to distinguish different ways of using language to organise or know our experiences. The details of his argument are not easy and much of the debate about his thesis has centred on this epistemological part of his case. These important issues cannot be explored here since our concern is with the justificatory part of his case. However, the central idea is fairly easy to grasp: all we need to do is to reflect on the rather different ways we would use language to express our knowledge of, say, why bacteria cause disease, of how we ought to behave, of Plato's arguments for the existence of the forms, and so on. In each case different ways of using language seem to be tied to different kinds of knowledge.

Hirst acknowledges difficulty in achieving a final, satisfactory specification of how the whole of human knowledge is to be seen as divisible into a limited number of forms, and there are important changes in detail between his several accounts. Such working adjustments do not threaten the general thesis, and for present purposes it will suffice to note the list given in *The Logic of Education*, written jointly with R. S. Peters (Hirst and Peters, 1970, pp. 63–4).

(1) *Formal logic and mathematics*. Truths here 'involve concepts that pick out relations of a general abstract kind, where deducibility within an axiom system is the particular test for truth'.

(2) *The physical sciences*. These 'are concerned with truths that, in the last analysis, stand or fall by the tests of observation by the senses'.

(3) *Awareness and understanding of our own and other people's minds*. Though it is far from clear how we are able to make judgements about other people's states of mind, it certainly is not a matter of straightforward observation as in the physical sciences. This form of understanding is not only evident in personal relationships, but also in history, psychology and sociology. (In some accounts Hirst classifies these as distinct forms.)

(4) *Moral judgements and awareness*. This is a distinct form of knowledge expressed through such concepts as 'ought', 'wrong' and 'duty', though the objectivity of moral judgements is debated.

(5) *Aesthetic experience*. In addition to language, this involves other forms of symbolic expression such as tone, form and colour.

(6) *Religious claims*. These are clearly not like other kinds of judgement, and it is debated whether there are objective grounds for them.

(7) *Philosophical understanding*. This involves unique 'second order' concepts, philosophy being a form of knowledge that seeks to understand the rational bases of other forms of knowledge.

It is important to bear in mind that Hirst is not inventing or recommending these forms of knowledge. He claims to be drawing attention to the kinds of knowledge that there actually are, and allowing the possibility that other forms may yet emerge and be recognised. This last concession may make the whole business sound rather arbitrary: for if new forms of knowledge can arise, what is so special about the ones we just happen to have at the moment? But two points should be noted. First, in learning to use language in ways appropriate to the various forms of knowledge we learn a 'public' language. We do not learn to use words in any way we like according to whims or fancy, but according to the public standards that give the language meaning. Other forms of knowledge could exist, but the ones we have did not just pop up: they emerged over millennia through the critical efforts of many generations to articulate their experience in language. Secondly, each of these distinctive ways of using language also has its distinctive way of testing propositions made in that language use, as is stated in Hirst's well-known table of four distinguishing features which mark off one form of knowledge from another (1974, p. 44).

(1) 'They each involve certain central concepts that are peculiar in character to the form.' (Hirst's examples are gravity, acceleration, hydrogen and photosynthesis in the sciences; God, sin and predestination in religion; ought, good and wrong in moral knowledge.)

(2) Each form 'has a distinctive logical structure'. For example, the terms and statements of mechanics can be meaningfully related in certain strictly limited ways only, and the same is true of historical explanation.

(3) 'Each form . . . has distinctive expressions that are testable

against experience in accordance with particular criteria that are peculiar to the form.'
(4) 'The forms have developed particular techniques and skills for exploring experience and testing their distinctive expressions.'

According to such a view, then, a liberal education will bring people to think in ways appropriate to the various forms of knowledge. This is not absurdly ambitious, as it may at first seem. For it is not proposed that pupils should learn all or even a great deal of what there is to be known within the various forms: only that they learn enough within each form to gain an understanding of the ways of thinking appropriate to it. Hirst does emphasise that 'this education will be one in the forms of knowledge themselves and not merely a self-conscious philosophical treatment of their characteristics. Scientific and historical knowledge are wanted, not knowledge of the philosophy of science and the philosophy of history' (ibid., p. 49). (In the light of these words it is hard to see why Mary Warnock should complain that 'on the Hirst theory of the curriculum, pupils will always be concerned with second-order subjects'; Warnock, 1977, p. 105).

In this way, then, Hirst re-maps the traditional notion of a liberal education while preserving it as an education that 'determined in scope and content by knowledge itself, is thereby concerned with the development of mind' (Hirst, 1974, p. 41). But such an education still needs to be justified and if he is not, for the moment, interested in any usefulness that the forms of knowledge may have, he must show why an education that develops the mind through the acquisition of knowledge is good in itself. To this end he uses a kind of argument known as a 'transcendental deduction'. Briefly, this is an argument that 'deduces' or justifies an answer by 'transcending' the question asked to show that an answer is already presupposed in the asking of that question. Thus he points out that anyone who asks for reasons why we should value the development of mind through the acquisition of knowledge must already value the pursuit of rational knowledge: for this is what his question is asking for. As he puts it:

To ask for the justification of any form of activity is significant only if one is in fact committed already to seeking rational knowledge. To ask for a justification of the pursuit of rational knowledge itself therefore presupposes some form of commitment to what one is seeking to justify. (ibid., p. 42)

We shall shortly consider R. S. Peters's fuller development of this kind of argument, which can be read as complementary to what Hirst says. For the present, therefore, I merely record that many philosophers do not find transcendental arguments persuasive. Meanwhile we should note that in certain practical respects Hirst's thesis is very attractive, some educators being drawn to it as a practical programme despite doubts about its philosophical base. Thus it can be reassuring to teachers troubled by persistent fears that they may omit to teach something important. For one who has a basic understanding of all the forms of knowledge is well equipped to master by himself any outstanding topic he may feel the need to know about. Furthermore, if what matters is to study enough from each particular form to ensure an understanding of the nature of that form, then ingenious curriculum-planners can select topics within each form which both exemplify the nature of that form and also have value for other reasons such as vocation or citizenship.

There are, however, important grounds for doubting the desirability of the sort of curriculum Hirst proposes. Thus R. K. Elliott in 'Education and human being' (1975) gives grounds for fearing that Hirst's curriculum would involve serious omissions and risk stifling or misdirecting pupils' initiatives. I shall discuss some of his main points in terms of three interdependent themes, *powers of the mind*, *critique of the disciplines* and *what matters most?*.

(1) *Powers of the mind*. Elliott denies that the development of powers of mind is only possible through forms of knowledge. Rather, forms of knowledge could never have developed if human beings did not already have powers to understand, retain, anticipate, seek clarity and so on. To neglect this is to overrate the element of convention embodied in human knowledge and to underrate the learner and his nature. There is more

48

in the progressive educator's talk of developing the child's natural potential than is allowed in Hirst's vision.

(2) *Critique of the disciplines.* Elliott says (1975, p. 58):

> The foundation of Hirst's doctrine is a logical classification of judgements by reference to their mode of validation. It does not matter, therefore, whether mathematics is derived from experience or not, or whether it is or is not applicable to experience. It is sufficient that it validates a logically distinct form of expression. That is considered sufficient reason why children should study mathematics throughout their school career.

But such formal characteristics alone do not guarantee educational worth. For this we must be able to show either that a discipline is a good means to develop the powers of mind or that it concerns things important for human beings to know about. 'It seems obvious that rigorous and systematic disciplines – Mathematics, Physics, History and Philosophy, for example – provide great scope for the exercise of the powers of understanding, and are about things that matter' (ibid., p. 59). Yet things are not so straightforward, for it is sometimes possible to approach the subject matter of a discipline without first learning that discipline. Further, the nature of the disciplines may be such that they have educational drawbacks offsetting their merits. Because the various disciplines have developed out of 'common' or 'everyday' understanding by treating their subject matters more rigorously and systematically, we naturally suppose they are superior ways of knowing about these subject matters. But this is doubtful. Should the unsystematic understanding of persons to be found in ordinary life or in imaginative literature be deprecated in favour of that afforded through systematic psychology or sociology? Can the study of art criticism be depended on to enrich pupils' aesthetic experience and bring them closer to the art work? We may get to know persons or works of art better without studying the relevant disciplines.

Similar doubts are appropriate to even the most esteemed disciplines. Thus science is widely assumed to tell us about physical reality. Yet,

In *The Crisis of the European Sciences*, Husserl suggests that since Galileo the motivation of Physics has undergone a gradual but massive change, chiefly owing to progressive idealisation; that the science no longer provides an understanding of the reality with which it was originally concerned; and that its own practitioners proceed for the most part technically and have only a technical understanding of what they are doing. (ibid., p. 60)

Behind these remarks lie difficult issues in the history of science. Briefly, the point is that we tend to think of natural science as telling us about physical reality because it is based on the rigorous and systematic observation of that reality. But rigorous observation of the history of science itself reveals how this view oversimplifies and misleads. Contrary to many bad histories, Galileo did not succeed just because he observed where others speculated. In fact, observation played a relatively small part in his work and he never disguised his cavalier way with inconvenient findings. More important was the thoroughgoing way in which he 'mathematicised' physics, turning the study of nature into a study of mathematical relationships. In subsequent centuries physicists have developed this approach to a point where experts in the field acknowledge difficulties about saying how their rigorously worked-out equations are related to the physical reality that is still assumed to be the subject matter of physics.

Whether or not we agree with these particular critiques of established disciplines, the important point is that such doubts can be raised about *any* discipline: so it is simply rash to go on assuming that mastery of a discipline necessarily improves our understanding of its subject matter. Rather, says Elliott:

These considerations suggest a task which properly belongs to Philosophy of Education, namely enquiry into the character of the disciplines with a view to assessing their educational value. It is less than just to give a student an education which encourages him to take enthusiastically to a discipline whose true character is not what it is proclaimed to be. In an extreme case he might be like a person who trains as a soldier in order to free the Holy Land, and,

> through nobody's fault, finds himself sacking Constantinople instead. Nor is it profitable for him to spend years of his life in arduous study when he would have been better advised to approach the objects studied, or supposedly studied, by the discipline not through the discipline itself but through common understanding. (ibid., pp. 61–2)

We should note the revolutionary implications of these points. It is often assumed that the job of the philosopher is not to reform disciplines like science, history, or mathematics, but merely to elucidate their nature, and that from such elucidation the educator is to draw conclusions about what should be taught and how. But a scrutiny of disciplines on the lines Elliott suggests must raise possibilities of reform. Scholars may not relish educational philosophers telling them how to study and advance their disciplines: yet if educational questions are to do with how bodies of knowledge can change and enrich people's understanding, thereby changing the kinds of persons they become, then it is regrettable that theorists have not responded to Elliott's suggestion that they develop a metacriticism of contemporary scholarship. I return to this theme in Chapter 3.

(3) *What matters most?* Elliott says that part of what makes it fitting that a person be educated is the importance of the things he comes to know. Disappointingly, he does not tell us how to estimate such importance. Yet surely he is right to suggest that in selecting curriculum content because it best exemplifies the logical features of a form of knowledge we risk neglecting the particular things that it is most important for people to know about. For example (not Elliott's), it might be judged that the best way to teach the nature of historical explanation would be to have students study some obscure backwater of history about which it is easier to achieve dispassionate objectivity precisely because it has no bearing on the modern world and is of little consequence to any overall vision of the human past. Much important historical knowledge would thus get left out. On this point Hirst himself says:

> Precisely what sections of the various disciplines are best suited to the aims of liberal education cannot be gone into

here. It is apparent that on philosophical grounds alone some branches of the sciences, for instance, would seem to be much more satisfactory as paradigms of scientific thinking than others. Many sections of physics are probably more comprehensive and clear in logical character, more typical of the well developed physical sciences than, say, botany. If so, they would, all other things being equal, serve better as an introduction to scientific knowledge. (Hirst, 1974, p. 49)

Elliott's misgivings about this approach are confirmed by some points made in John Passmore's *Science and its Critics* (1978). Passmore describes a hierarchy in the world of science whereby great esteem is afforded to those areas of research which are regarded as typically scientific because they achieve the most thorough-going mathematical abstraction.

At the top of the hierarchy stand mathematical physicists, who take as their ideal the discovery of such equations as $e = mc^2$, which make no reference to any particular entities. Next come those scientists who work with entities – genes, molecules, electrons – which are 'theoretical' in the sense that we take them to exist and to behave in particular ways only as a consequence of accepting a set of scientific theories. Through a set of intermediate sciences which make use of such general formulae and such theoretical entities in the analysis of more accessible phenomena – earthquakes or disease – we pass finally to what is often dismissed as 'natural history', the detailed description of phenomena in terms of their 'everyday' properties. (Passmore, 1978, p. 52)

Accordingly researchers are discouraged from inquiring into difficult or less elegant phenomena. Yet,

Geologists like Lyell, biologists like Darwin, physiologists like Harvey, psychologists like Freud and Piaget, sociologists like Marx and Max Weber have done at least as much, without the help of theoretical entities or mathematics, to transform our knowledge of ourselves and of

the world as ever did Galileo and Newton and Einstein . . .
To put them at the bottom of an intellectual pecking order
is merely arrogant. (ibid., p. 53)

And if science itself suffers when too much value is set on areas
of research that best exemplify the supposedly distinctive
nature of science, then Hirst's curriculum recommendations
could be similarly damaging.

Like points would hold for other forms of knowledge. Thus
Hirst says: 'Perhaps in literature and the fine arts the paradigm
principle is less easy to apply though probably many would
favour a course in literature to any one other' (1974, p. 49). But
surely very few people *would* regard literature as the paradigm
art form. A common view is that formal qualities are centrally
distinctive of the aesthetic as such, and these are most explicit
and undiluted in arts like music and abstract painting. This is
the view behind Walter Pater's assertion that 'All art constantly
aspires towards the condition of music' (Pater, 1961, p. 129) and
Clive Bell's influential theory of 'significant form' (Bell, 1914).
On such views 'pure' art forms like music and abstract painting
would best suit Hirst's educational purpose. Literature might
be judged a poor exemplar of a distinctively aesthetic way of
understanding because of its important non-aesthetic ingredients such as moral and psychological insights. But these,
surely, are reasons for giving literature a very special educational value that Hirst's formal criteria will omit.

R. S. Peters

Rather late in this book we can now attend to the discussions of
our problem by R. S. Peters who, more than any other contemporary writer, has brought it into the forum of educational debate under its now familiar formulation as the problem of 'worthwhileness of activities'. That Peters should concern himself
with this problem is appropriate to his contention that 'education' *means* coming to know and care for activities that are
valued for their own sake. He has made several attacks on the
problem but the first in the 'Worthwhile activities' chapter of
Ethics and Education (1966) is still the best known and most
discussed. I shall attempt to summarise the difficult central

arguments, notwithstanding Peters's own subsequent doubts about them. (People do sometimes abandon correct views!) An important later treatment, 'The justification of education' (1973), is too difficult to summarise in an introductory text, though I shall refer to part of it.

In *Ethics and Education* Peters first considers two approaches to the problem that have already been explored in this book. He finds them wanting but thinks they contain important points. The utilitarian emphasis on pleasure is mistaken as it stands, but reminds us that if human beings did not have desires the satisfaction of which gave pleasure, then they would never have had any reason to do anything and the idea of acting for reasons would never have developed. Aristotle's teleological view is also mistaken but rightly attempts to justify the good life for man by appealing to his use of reason. The correct way to do this is not to argue from man's supposed *telos* but to make reason the starting point for an argument by transcendental deduction (the kind of argument we have already seen used by Hirst).

A transcendental argument 'attempts to make explicit what a person is committed to who makes use of his reason in attempting to answer the question "What ought I to do?"' (Peters, 1966, p. 153). Peters contends that questions like 'What ought I to do?' and 'Why do this rather than that?' can be seriously asked only by people who sees things in a certain way and who already have certain commitments. If we can discern those presuppositions they will point towards an answer.

First, then, to be able to ask 'Why do this rather than that?' one must be able to see that there are considerations intrinsic to activities themselves which constitute reasons for pursuing them. Some people are strangers to this attitude and can only ask questions about whether some activity is good as a means to something else, usually something else to do with what Plato called the satisfaction of the basic appetites. But one who asks the question has learned to look at activities for themselves, and this being so, he must be aware that particular activities can be appraised because of the standards immanent in them rather than because of what they lead on to. For how could one have learned to value activities for their own sake except by participating in activities which had their own standards of excellence?

In different ways different activities come to involve different standards of, say, elegance, ingenuity, shrewdness, appropriateness, neatness, or cogency. As we participate in such activities, we begin to respond to such standards and become aware that the activity can have a value in its own right. Thus a primitive man might go hunting simply because he needs food. As he becomes a good hunter, achieving skill, speed and style in pursuing his prey, he will find satisfaction in achieving these standards. A day will come when he chooses to go hunting to exercise his skill, speed and style, even though his larder is full. Standards in the activity have made it possible to value that activity for its own sake.

So we can take it, suggests Peters, that our questioner will give his preference to activities which give scope for the achievement of standards. Furthermore, since activities go on for some time, he must prefer those which do not threaten boredom: those which are likely to hold his interest because they afford him 'rich opportunities for employing his wits, resources and sensitivities in situations in which there is a premium on unpredictability and opportunities for skill' (Peters, 1966, p. 167). All this relates to the ways in which human beings have transformed activities that originally involved no more than the satisfaction of basic appetites such as those for food and sex and warmth. Elaborate norms of gastronomy, courtship, dress and house-building have come to govern the way we satisfy such needs: norms and conventions which gave scope to exercise skill, taste, sensibility and the like, so making it possible for people to find them worthwhile in their own right.

A further point is that the various activities a man chooses must be such as can fit coherently into his life as a whole: one cannot seriously choose mutually incompatible activities.

But Peters is not satisfied with the arguments so far, for nothing in them shows that the pursuit of science or art is any more worthwhile than playing golf or bridge: both kinds of activities have built-in standards, are always opening up new possibilities and are mutually compatible. Science and art seem, so far, to be no more nor less worthwhile than the best games. Yet 'science or philosophy or history are manifestly not just pastimes' and what matters is 'the character which they share over and above what they have in common with games and pastimes' (ibid., p. 158). To get at this extra something Peters elucidates a second group of presuppositions lying behind 'Why do this rather than that?' questions. The point of the 'why' here is, of course, to ask for reasons and, if the question is serious, for valid or true reasons. Now, in their various ways, what Peters has called 'serious activities' all yield knowledge that is relevant to answering the question posed. Studies like history, science, philosophy and literature all help us to form a view of ourselves and of our world, and so of the kind of activities we might pursue in that world.

Two brief examples may help to illustrate the sort of thing he is getting at here. The study of history throws some light on questions about what things are worth doing, because it shows us something of the diversity of human pursuits in different ages and the diversity of values men have found in them. And recent developments in various branches of science have suggested very different accounts of what is actually going on when a human being creates a work of art, explores the earth's surface, and so on. Accordingly Peters can say of our questioner:

> When he stands back and reflects about what it is that he is doing he then engages in the sorts of activities of which the curriculum of a university is largely constructed. He will find himself embarking upon those forms of inquiry such as science, history, literature and philosophy which are concerned with the description, explanation, and assessment of different forms of human activity. It would be irrational for a person who seriously asks himself the question 'Why do this rather than that?' to close his mind arbitrarily to any form of inquiry which might throw light on the question which he is asking. (ibid., pp. 162–3)

So anyone who wants to know what is worth doing must think it is worth pursuing those kinds of knowledge which promise to illumine the question. Yet there is still a problem, for, Peters notes, it might be said that this is an argument only for the *instrumental* value of 'serious activities'. To show that such activities should be pursued to help answer a question is not to show that they should be pursued for their own sake, though it may be that we have reached a point where it is inappropriate to distinguish between intrinsic and instrumental worth. 'Thinking scientifically for instance, is not exactly instrumental to answering the question "Why do this rather than that?"; for it transforms the question by transforming how "this" and "that" are conceived' (ibid., pp. 163–4).

That science and other serious activities should have this transforming power derives from another aspect of their seriousness not yet noted. They are serious because they are tied to 'man's curiosity about the world and his awe and concern about his own particular predicament in it' (ibid., p. 164). They share in the concern for truth that is also present when a man seriously asks questions about what he should do. For,

> In so far as he can stand back from his life and *ask* the question 'Why this rather than that?' he must already have a serious concern for truth built into his consciousness. For how can a serious practical question be asked unless a man also wants to acquaint himself as well as he can of the situation out of which the question arises and of the facts of various kinds which provide the framework for possible answers? The various theoretical inquiries are explorations of these different facets of his experience. To ask the question 'Why do this rather than that?' seriously is therefore, however embryonically, to be committed to those inquiries which are defined by their serious concern with those aspects of reality which give context to the question which he is asking. In brief the justification of such activities is not purely instrumental because they are involved in *asking* the question 'Why do this rather than that?' as well as in answering it. (loc. cit.)

If the reader has difficulty grasping this last move in the argument he may find help in the paper 'The justification of education' (1973) where Peters says something more about why he thinks truth and rationality are among the ultimate human values: why, like happiness, they have value in themselves and not for any consequences they may yield. There Peters comments on the possibility that someone might doubt the value of justification itself: 'The difficulty about querying the value of justification is that any such query, if it is not frivolous, presupposes its value. For to discuss its value is immediately to embark upon reasons for or against it, which is itself a further example of justification' (Peters, 1973, p. 253). Non-philosophers often get impatient about arguments like this, finding them more clever than helpful. But Peters thinks it is an important argument. It points to the fact that the demand for reason and the search for justification is something inescapable in human life. It brings home to us something important about man.

> For human beings do not just veer towards goals like moths towards a light; they are not just programmed by an instinctive equipment. They conceive of ends, deliberate about them and about the means to them. They follow rules and revise and assess them . . .
>
> Man is thus a creature who lives under the demands of reason. He can, of course, be unreasonable or irrational; but these terms are only intelligible as fallings short in respect of reason . . . the demands of reason are not just an option available to the reflective. (ibid., p. 254)

Human life, in other words, is inescapably a matter of making assessments and trying to get things right, so that reason, truth and knowledge are necessarily among things human beings value, just as are happiness and pleasure. An argument from the nature of knowledge turns out to be, in part at least, an argument about the nature of man.

If we now attempt some assessment of Peters's arguments we encounter a peculiar difficulty consequent on the fact that he argues by transcendental deduction. A remarkable thing about transcendental deductions is that many philosophers, including some who use them, find no flaw in their logic yet confess to serious unease about them. There is, after all, something disconcerting about arguments that derive powerful justifications from the fact that a question has been asked. Of course, hunches and feelings must never pass for refutations; but they do have a place in philosophy. For philosophical progress is often achieved when hunches are followed up by careful analysis which may make explicit what had only been vaguely sensed.

Much philosophical work needs to be done on the subject of transcendental deductions and their various uses. Meanwhile, three more specific points about Peters's arguments should be noted.

(1) In choosing a curriculum, we have to judge which disciplines are more worthy of study and also what is most worth knowing within each discipline. Now, at the stage of his argument where Peters says that the various kinds of knowledge available to man must be evaluated for the light they throw on possible options, his case would point to answers to both questions. The knowledge that is most illuminating would be rated highest. However, we saw that Peters would not rest here and went on to argue for a general commitment to truth and rationality. It is hard to see how such a conclusion could give any help in the details of curriculum selection. Many of the earlier criticisms of Hirst's theory are again pertinent.

(2) Another difficulty emerges if we consider the case of a man who cares greatly for one of what Peters calls 'serious activities'. Confronted with Peters's deduction he may find no fault with it. The argument might strike him as impeccable, yet have nothing to do with why he cares for science, history, literature, or whatever. There can hardly have been any systematic research on the matter, yet it is reasonable to believe that if large numbers of people who cared passionately for 'serious activities' were to 'search their breasts' for the grounds of this care, then very few would find themselves motivated by the same concern for truth and rationality that is presupposed in the desire to know whether and why we should do anything. Our present concerns might be a case in point: those of us who puzzle over the philosophy of the curriculum beyond the demands of examinations and certification presumably do so because we think that the questions involved are interesting or important in some specific way, not because this is one possible way to display a commitment to truth and rationality.

Of course, it could be that for various very personal reasons people pursue activities that are also susceptible of more general justification. But if the grounds of such general justification are remote from considerations that have led intelligent and sensitive persons to pursue activities with energy and passion, then should we not suspect that a justification in Peters's general terms cannot touch many of the values these activities have for man? As Elliott puts it, 'it is because he loves poetry that a critic seeks the truth of poems rather than of other things; if he valued poems simply as occasions for actualising his general love of knowledge he would not be a lover of poetry at all' (Elliott, 1977, p. 13).

(3) Finally, there is something misleading about the way Peters presents the problem. To talk of someone seriously asking 'why do this rather than that?' seems to ignore the passionate urgency with which we are liable to be engrossed in these pursuits, to be 'caught' by them rather than choose them after calm deliberation. It is almost as if Peters would have us picture someone whose life is all in order, devoid of puzzles, problems and outstanding responsibilities except in so far as he now has time on his hands which he wishes to use in a justifiable way; and that he now asks whether and why he should devote these spare hours to pushpin or poetry, to skittles or scholarship. Yet part of the point of Peters's insistence on the seriousness of serious activities is that they are not just pleasing embellishments added to life, but are somehow part of what life is, or ought to be, all about. We need, it seems, to refer to more than knowledge and rationality to work out why this should be.

IV Religious Answers

Readers may wonder that I have so long deferred considering the kind of answer to which I now turn; for many people find in religion a source of guidance on all problems about how we should live and what we should value. Typically, of course, religion is a matter of believing in, and relating to, a divine being: a fitting object of worship who is of supreme power and goodness. Such beliefs being thought to bear on all questions about the conduct of our lives, religious doctrines can be expected to tell us the proper place of learning and culture in the good life.

Clearly, this discussion cannot attend satisfactorily to even the major religions and their associated views of the good life, let alone the diversity of interpretations within these. But attention to some thinkers from two closely related religions will pinpoint some of the possible issues involved.

For the early fathers of the Christian church the problem of what learning to foster was a pressing one, arising in the following way. The Christian belief was that the supremely important thing for man is to come to know and love God: the appropriate knowledge being available to him by revelation in Holy Scripture, the testimony of which is to be accepted by faith. Accordingly many early Christians denied the value of 'high-culture' and any but the minimal learning: such things seemed to be irrelevant indulgences deflecting attention from men's proper concerns. However, Christianity was an evangelising faith in a world where many people were highly educated in the pagan culture of Greece and Rome. Christian teachers therefore felt a need to study the pagan learning of those whom they sought to convert; and many converts to Christianity brought their pagan learning with them. It became evident that pagan learning and Christian culture were by no means incompatible in every respect and some Christians came to think that there were respects in which pagan culture could strengthen and enrich Christian ideals. Two opposed views which thus emerged within Christianity are nicely summarised in some quotations from the early Christian fathers that are juxtaposed in Howie's study of St Augustine's educational thought (1969b). The view that there could be nothing of Christian value in pagan culture is well put by St Jerome:

> What communication can there be between light and darkness? What common ground between Christ and Belial? What has Horace to do with the Psalms? Or Vergil with the Gospels? Or Cicero with the Apostle Paul? – We should not at one and the same time drink the cup of Christ and the cup of evil spirits. (Quoted in Howie, 1969a, p. 218)

Such views have, of course, had lasting influence among some Christians. The opposed doctrine is put by St Clement:

> There is one river of Truth, but many streams fall into it on this side and that – I call him truly learned who brings

everything to bear on the truth so that, gathering what is useful from geometry and music and philosophy itself, he guards the faith against assault. (Quoted in ibid., p. 219)

The debate between these two viewpoints had become urgent by the time of the great fourth-century Christian philosopher St Augustine of Hippo. Augustine's own life and conversion, as recorded in his *Confessions*, put him in a position from which to appreciate the strength of both views. Born of a Christian mother and pagan father he did not at first take his Christian instruction very seriously but followed the standard education of a well-to-do Roman provincial. Accidentally, however, this set him on the road to Christian conversion: for, to improve himself as a public speaker, he studied the great Latin stylist Cicero. But as well as elegant prose, he found in Cicero a call to study philosophy and seek wisdom. He responded eagerly, and his life was profoundly changed. He sought wisdom from many sources and creeds; and he records how studies in secular culture both blocked and facilitated his path to Christianity. His acquired taste for elegant writing rendered the Bible distasteful to him; but the study of Greek philosophy liberated him from materialistic prejudices and made the idea of God easier to accept. In time he became rationally persuaded of the truth of Christianity but emotionally unable to embrace the faith; complete acceptance being achieved at last not by learning but by what he took to be divine intervention. Augustine concluded that secular learning could be both aid and obstacle to Christian enlightenment. It could start someone on the quest and help him along the way, though on its own it could never be sufficient to bring a man to God. Further, he saw much in secular education as pointless or worse, complaining of his own schooling for example:

I was obliged to memorize the wanderings of a hero named Aeneas, while in the meantime I failed to remember my own erratic ways. I learned to lament the death of Dido, who killed herself for love, while all the time, in the midst of these things, I was dying, separated from you, my God and my Life, and I shed no tears for my own plight.
What can be more pitiful than an unhappy wretch

unaware of his own sorry state, bewailing the fate of Dido, who died for love of Aeneas, yet shedding no tears for himself as he dies for want of loving you? (Augustine, 1961, I, 13, pp. 33–4)

Of course, we could reply that Augustine here overlooked the many ways in which the real or imaginary life of another can importantly illumine our own lives. But this would miss the main point: that Augustine evaluated all possible learning exclusively by reference to his religious view of the ends of human life. Indeed, he thought there was something reprehensibly indulgent about ideas of liberal education as the pursuit of knowledge for its own sake. There were more important things to do with our minds than use them to indulge idle curiosity. Later on, as Bishop of Hippo, Augustine had to administer programmes of Christian education, and so examined systematically the problem of pagan elements in Christian schooling. In 'On Christian education' he is explicit: Christians do not have the monopoly of wisdom, and there are many pagans whose penetrating vision contains important insights into the nature of things. Christian educators should use anything in the pagan traditions that will serve their cause.

If those who are called philosophers, especially the Platonists, have said anything which is true and in harmony with our faith, we should not shrink from it, but appropriate it to our own use, as though we were taking it from people who were in unlawful possession of it. (Quoted Howie, 1969a, p. 209)

This historically important resolution helped to establish an enduring tradition of broadly based Christian scholarship. For from a perspective such as this there are a number of ways in which an educator might see learning that is not specifically religious as yet contributing to religious understanding. Versions of each of the following five suggestions are to be found among the voluminous writings of St Augustine and other early Christian educators.

(1) Some knowledge of the culture, language and geography of biblical peoples is necessary in order to understand the

scriptures. And an evangelising Christian needs some such knowledge of the peoples he is to evangelise.

(2) Some doctrines arrived at by pagans are compatible with, and reinforce, Christian teachings: for example, Plato's theory of the immortal soul.

(3) The pursuit of learning is an entry into the world of ideas whereby we become less susceptible to a materialistic and anti-religious vision.

(4) Learning pursues and achieves truth. But the presence of truth in the world, and man's capacity to enjoy truth, is God-given. In achieving truth we relate to God.

(5) Learning about and understanding the world that God has created is a way of worshipping God: especially in so far as the discovery of an order in nature confirms God's existence.

On such grounds as these, then, it is possible to give a religious justification for a broadly based curriculum, educating students into all the main areas of human inquiry and achievement. (Augustine himself allowed virtually no place for the arts in education: but looking back on a cultural history in which the arts have often served religion, we can see that this exclusion need not follow.) And if a curriculum is planned on such a basis, this will determine not only the selection of subject matter but also the way in which subject matter is understood and taught.

A thorough-going present-day commitment to such a pervasively religious curriculum is found among Muslim philosophers of education, as is evidenced in the various contributions to the World Conference on Muslim Education held at Mecca in 1977 (al-Attas, 1979).

These philosophers criticise Western culture and education on the grounds that, lacking any higher aim, the Western secular-rational approach to learning has degenerated into the endless and insatiable pursuit of more and more knowledge. Thus according to the editor of the collection the various faculties of Western universities engage in discrete pieces of research unrelated to any unifying vision:

Like a man with no personality, the modern university has no abiding, vital centre, no permanent underlying prin-

64

ciple establishing its final purpose. It still pretends to contemplate the universal and even claims to possess faculties and departments as if it were the body of an organ – but it has no brain, let alone intellect and soul, except only in terms of a purely administrative function of maintenance and physical development. Its development is not guided by a *final* principle and definite purpose, except by the relative principle urging on the pursuit of knowledge incessantly, with no absolute end in view. (al-Attas, 1979, pp. 38–9)

Western educational thought likewise evidences this failure to inform education with a grasp of central values. One contributor, Syed Ali Ashraf, distinguishes two main philosophies in Western education. 'Secular-modernists' such as John Vaizey are so preoccupied with change that they entirely neglect the need for education to be a conserver of human values. And 'humanists' such as R. S. Peters 'conceive education as a continuous process of mental, emotional and moral development, as initiation into a quality of life which helps man to see different points of view and the relationship of these various points of view to one another'. But 'The unfortunate thing about this attitude is its vagueness. It considers education as having "no ends beyond itself". It makes a person, as Newman rightly pointed out, "a gentleman" and not necessarily a "religious man". The spiritual world or the world after death does not have any relevance to the process of cultivating this quality' (al-Attas, 1979, p. xi).

In contrast to such approaches, 'religion provides an all-comprehensive norm of man and an all-inclusive goal for education . . . According to religion this goal is revealed to man and thus it has an objective status. It is not concocted by man or just derived from experience' (ibid., p. xii). 'One great advantage that this concept has over the humanistic concept is that it provides a supreme ideal and an unshakable norm for educationists to aim at when they are planning the education system and working out the methodology' (ibid., p. xiii). For as Ahmad Salah Jamjoom puts it in the foreword: 'The aim of Muslim education is the creation of the "good and righteous man" who worships Allah in the true sense of the term, builds up the structure of his earthly life according to the *sharia* [Islamic law] and employs it to subserve his faith' (ibid., p. v).

Various contributors spell out aspects of how this vision is to be translated into practice. The concern will be to enable man to understand Allah and Allah's ways in the universe he has created. To this end a wide range of subjects will be studied but in a thoroughly Islamic perspective, as Jamjoom makes clear:

> In the Islamic sense science is a form of worship by which man is brought into closer contact with Allah; hence it should not be abused to corrupt faith and morals and to bring forth harm, corruption, injustice and aggression.
>
> Consequently any science which is in conflict with faith and which does not serve its ends and requirements is in itself corrupt, and stands condemned and rejected and has no place in God's injunctions. (ibid., p. vi)

Accordingly, Muhammad Qutb argues, the sciences are to be taught as 'spiritual journeys . . . into God's miraculous phenomena' (ibid., p. 57) and 'autonomous' disciplines are to be studied only by those already equipped with a sound knowledge of Islam. The corruption of scholarship by atheism, agnosticism, or religions other than Islam is to be positively resisted.

Of course, many more writers than those I have noted have based their educational philosophies on their religious convictions, and their conclusions have been many and diverse. The selections I have made may not be typical but they have, I hope, been suitable to bring out five points as follows.

(1) It is likely that a religious educational theorist will find in his religion grounds for valuing an education in the great areas of human knowledge and creativity.

(2) He will, however, value these for their instrumental rather than their intrinsic worth, though it will be a very special kind of instrumental worth.

(3) Accordingly, his religious purposes will be reflected in the way he would have the various subjects studied, perhaps to the point of transforming them.

66

(4) He may too be very selective of the actual subject matters to be studied, perhaps excluding bodies of thought that challenge his religious commitment.

(5) On the other hand, it is quite possible for a religious person to contend that the immediacy and overwhelming importance of religious experience is such that cultural pursuits are a frivolous irrelevancy or distraction.

So while it is to be anticipated that a man's religious views will make a difference to how he thinks about education, precisely *what* difference it will make is far from clear. A determinate prescription does not seem to follow from the fact of belief in God. Rather, very different views can be developed in the light of such a belief. A religious person cannot simply turn to his religion to tell him what to include in the curriculum. If he is serious he will have to go through deliberations like those in this book, though the way he does this will be informed to an important extent by his religion.

There is, of course, a more obvious difficulty about turning to religion for an answer to educational puzzles. Typically nowadays education takes place in communities of people with mixed religious convictions, so there are clear objections to using religious doctrines as a basis for selecting a curriculum for all; especially if, as we have seen can happen, this is done in a restrictive and doctrinaire way. However, in Chapter 3 I shall propose a view that incorporates something of what is contended by the Muslim educators whom I have discussed. Sympathetic to their complaints that Western education lacks a unifying purpose to do with how we see and live our lives, I shall argue the possibility of achieving such a purpose without imposing one dogma and sacrificing liberal principles of open inquiry.

V Views that Educators Cannot or Should Not Make Judgements of Worthwhileness

We have considered various doctrines as to how educators should judge what knowledge is to be taught for its intrinsic worth. Notwithstanding their considerable merits, none has been found entirely satisfactory. We might therefore draw one or both of two conclusions:

(1) That no rational answer is possible: that the choice of what things are worthwhile for their own sakes is just a matter of personal preference or feeling, incapable of being objectively evaluated or supported by reasons.

(2) That educators ought not to make such choices on behalf of pupils; for to do so is to impose an arbitrary personal preference. Not the teacher but the learner should choose what to learn.

These two views are the subject of this section.

View 1: That There Can Be No Rational Basis for Choice

This is a version of a view of values that has been variously elaborated by a number of theorists and is also expressed in the assertions of many laymen that questions of right and wrong, good or bad, are matters of feeling, not of fact. Thus the eighteenth-century Scots philosopher David Hume could see no way in which reason could decide between different value judgements, and concluded that our feelings must decide such matters. Fortunately, he believed, most people have a 'moral sentiment' which makes them prefer the well-being to the suffering of their fellows; but if someone does not share this preference, there can be no persuading him by reason nor any demonstrating if he is right or wrong. For moral judgements are neither judgements of fact nor of reason: they are expressions of how we feel. And the same is true of all judgements of value.

The best-known modern statement in English of this emotivist view was made in 1936 by A. J. Ayer who had been working with a group of philosophers known as the Vienna Circle or the Logical Positivists. These thinkers were impressed by what they took to be the sound foundations of some areas of inquiry, particularly the natural sciences (where true and false judgements can be distinguished by empirical observation) and mathematics (where true and false judgements can be distinguished by analysis and demonstration). But they contended that in other areas, such as religion and values, there could be no knowledge because here there were no ways of distinguishing true from false judgements. Such judgements were neither true nor false but meaningless, for the famous verification principle of the logical positivists asserts that any proposition which cannot be verified is meaningless.

Accordingly, Ayer and others held that the realm of ethics and value judgements is not an area of knowledge at all, and that when we make value judgements we are not making statements of fact: we are expressing our feelings. As Ayer puts it, a sentence like 'stealing money is wrong' sounds like a statement of fact; but it has no factual meaning, for despite its propositional form it contains no proposition which can be verified, which can be either true or false.

> It is as if I had written 'Stealing money!!' – where the shape and thickness of the exclamation marks show, by a suitable convention, that a special sort of moral disapproval is the feeling which is being expressed. It is clear that there is nothing said here which can be true or false. Another man may disagree with me about the wrongness of stealing, in the sense that he may not have the same feelings about stealing as I have, and he may quarrel with me on account of my moral sentiments. But he cannot, strictly speaking, contradict me. For in saying that a certain type of action is right or wrong, I am not making any factual statement, not even a statement about my own state of mind. I am merely expressing certain moral sentiments. And the man who is ostensibly contradicting me is merely expressing his moral sentiments. So that there is plainly no sense in asking which of us is in the right. For neither of us is asserting a genuine proposition. (Ayer, 1971, pp. 142–3)

Ayer believes this analysis holds for all realms of value judgements, so that if it is correct it precludes reasoning about the value of knowledge and its place in education: this book is condemned to failure from the start. Indeed, two influential works in philosophy of education (Hardie, 1962; O'Connor,

1957) do take this view and abstain from discussing curriculum values. There are, however, reasons why few philosophers accept an emotivist view of values. I shall discuss three of these.

(1) Sometimes our feelings do not coincide with our value judgements, as when we say 'I want to do that although I know it is wrong' or 'I know it's good but I don't like it'. This does not seem to fit with the view that our value judgements are always expressions of our emotions. (Some emotivists say that what we really have in these cases is a conflict of two emotions: the reader must judge the persuasiveness of this reply.)

(2) The theory suggests that we make value judgements about things because we have certain feelings or emotions towards them. But this is an oversimple view of emotions. For if we feel emotions of approval or disapproval towards something, we can ask ourselves *why* we feel this way about it; and often we can give an answer. Furthermore, our emotions towards things often change as we come to see or understand them in new ways: as, for example, when we learn new things about persons or works of art. It seems that our value judgements cannot be straightforward expressions of our emotions. In part at least, our emotions express our judgements: they are based on reasons.

(3) Much of the emotivist case is only negative in an important way. To show that we cannot test the truth of value judgements in the way that we can test judgements in science or mathematics is not to show that they cannot be judged true or false in ways appropriate to their subject matter. We cannot here explore the works of philosophers who have sought to show just this possibility: though Hirst's contention that there are seven or eight forms of knowledge is relevant. The important point is that the emotivist has not shown that there *cannot* be other kinds of knowledge: that there *cannot* be reasoning about values. And this book will conclude with an attempt to show that judgements about the worth of knowledge are not just matters of feeling; that they can be called before the bar of reason.

View 2: That Educators Ought Not To Make Judgements of Worthwhileness on Behalf of their Pupils

This view is typically associated with that broad body of educational attitudes usually known as 'child-centred', 'progressive', or 'free'. A systematic discussion of the associated ideas is difficult because they belong to a varied and still-evolving movement. Furthermore, campaigning practical reformers have rarely had the time and energy to elaborate a carefully argued case. However, we can detect two main grounds for believing that the ultimate choice of what is worth studying is to be made by pupils. I will label these (*a*) the natural growth view and (*b*) the rights view.

(*a*) *The natural growth view* involves seeing education and the development of a child's mind in terms of a metaphor: though a metaphor that advocates intend us to take very literally. Education is to be conceived on the model of the growth and nurture of a plant. The teacher should tend his pupils as the wise gardener tends his plants, providing for them the most helpful environment and nourishment, but never trying to do their growing for them, nor to have them become anything other than it is in their nature to become. Accordingly, what and when the child shall learn is to be determined by the child's own nature, just as the nature of an acorn determines it to grow into a tree and not a cabbage.

Use of this metaphor dates back at least to Plato; but it made its big reforming impact following the publication of Rousseau's *Emile* in 1762. This book is mainly a fictionalised account of the ideal education of one child. Clearly aware of absurd impracticalities in much that he describes, Rousseau intended to offer not a manual of pedagogical prescriptions but an invocation to see things in a new way. He asserted the unique worth of the individual as an autonomous person judging things for himself and shaping his own life. Yet, he thought, people failed to achieve such fulfilment due to oppressive political institutions, an oversophisticated culture and restrictive educational practices. The last stifled independent thought and imposed abstract knowledge foreign to the child's nature. Rousseau's remedy was an education that did not stunt and corrupt the child's mind by imposing from above, but allowed the free development of thought and personality from within. In propagandising this vision, he sometimes used the growth metaphor, though never developing it fully or making it central to his thought. This was done by the nineteenth-century Prussian educator Friedrich Froebel. Much that Froebel says is difficult, if not impossibly obscure; but the following much-quoted passage from *The Education of Man* is clear enough:

> To young plants and animals we give space and time, knowing that then they will grow correctly according to inherent law; we give them rest and avoid any violent interference such as disturbs healthy growth. But the human being is regarded as a piece of wax or a lump of clay which can be moulded into any shape we choose. Why is it that we close our minds to the lesson which Nature silently teaches? Wild plants which grow where they are crowded and confined scarcely suggest any shape of their own, but if we see them growing freely in the fields we can then observe their ordered life and form – a sun's shape, a radiant star, springs from the earth. So children who are early forced by their parents into a pattern and purpose unsuited to their nature might have grown in beauty and in the fullness of their powers.
>
> If we take account of divine action and consider man in his original state, it is clear that all teaching which pre-scribes and determines must impede, destroy, annihilate.
> (Quoted in Lilley, 1967, p. 52)

Equally clear is the statement made by Edmond Holmes in *What Is and What Might Be* (1911), a book now largely forgotten but once a great motivator of educational change.

> If the potencies of our nature are not worth realising we had better give up the business of living. If they are we had better fall into line with other living things . . .
>
> The perfect manhood which is present in embryo in the new-born infant, just as the oak-tree is present in embryo in the acorn, will struggle unceasingly to evolve itself.
> (Holmes, 1911, p. 241)

According to such views, then, it is the child's nature that should determine what the child is to learn; and the way to secure this is to let the child choose. If the child ought to learn what is according to his nature, and if his choices will reflect his nature, then he will choose to learn that which is right for him to learn.

(b) *The rights view* is a central theme in the thought of A. S. Neill, the much-publicised reforming head of Summerhill School who is widely but wrongly regarded as a typical child-centred educationist. Neill was a maverick among progressivist educators, objecting to their high moral tone and never even reading the growth theorists. His view seems to have been that it was an inadmissable presumption for adults to decide whether or what a child is to learn: if a child wants to study he will do so in his own good time, and if he does not want to, then no one is justified in compelling him. Accordingly he provided study opportunities at Summerhill but let students decide whether to use them. On principle he would not experiment with new curricula and teaching methods to entice children to more attractive lessons.

More recently, similar views have been associated with assertions that the institutional nature of schools is such that there is likely to be something sinister about what is chosen to go into the curriculum. 'De-schoolers' and exponents of the 'New' sociology of knowledge both suggest that state schools are administered by authorities concerned to preserve the social order. Accordingly, it is charged, they will choose curricula to make children accept that order rather than understand and criticise it. Moreover, children from one social group studying a curriculum chosen by members of another group will find it alien and difficult, thus becoming ashamed of their own cultural background and doubting their own intellectual competence. Such aberrations are said to be inevitable when one group chooses what others are to study.

Views such as these have generated important debates involving issues beyond the scope of this book. Many have found them persuasive and others have rejected them while allowing that they have motivated educational improvements. But there are reasons for believing that it would be disastrous if educators were swayed by such arguments to abdicate making judgements of educational worth. Three of these are as follows.

(1) The growth metaphor is fundamentally misleading. The way a mind changes when it is educated is essentially unlike the way a plant changes as it grows. For the knowledge, beliefs, skills and attitudes we acquire in becoming educated are in no sense natural acquisitions. Rather they are human artefacts: the components of a culture that men have created through generations. Education is an unnatural activity through which teachers exercise considerable influence over the kinds of persons their pupils become. If teachers abdicate this unnatural power over the child, they do not thereby leave him free to develop naturally: they leave him even more subject to other unnatural influences from the social environment – some of them potentially malicious.

(2) I have quoted Froebel's invocation to let children's minds grow like plants according to the laws of their nature. But Froebel goes on to say: 'The vine has to be pruned, but pruning as such does not bring more wine; however good the intention, the vine may be entirely ruined in the process or its fertility destroyed unless the gardener pays attention to the plant's natural growth' (quoted in Lilley, 1967, p. 52). Holmes too acknowledges that man is unique in having acquired self-consciousness and the 'power of interfering, for good or ill, with the spontaneous energies of our nature' (Holmes, 1911, p. 242). But these points have implications beyond what the writers allow, for they require the educator to develop a view of the child's nature. The provision of any environment where the child is to grow 'naturally' is itself bound to be selective. Froebelians carefully furnish their appropriately named *Kindergartens* so as to foster the growth they see as appropriate. Neill let his pupils choose whether to attend classes; but they could choose history or science, not witchcraft or karate. It is instructive to compare a range of growth theorists. Rousseau, Froebel, Holmes, Rudolph Steiner and the Plowden Committee all had different visions of the child's nature and of where 'natural growth' is to lead; which is hardly surprising, in view of the points made in Section II of this chapter ('Naturalistic theories of justification', p. 13) regarding the problems of specifying human nature. There can be no 'neutral' provision

for the child's nature to flower. Nor can these problems be avoided by reinterpreting the growth theories not according to their literal wording, but according to a theme in the context of ideas from which they emerged. In his excellent description of this context, Charles Taylor shows how Romantic thinkers evolved a view of life as self-expression or fulfilment (Taylor, 1975, ch. 1). By this they meant nothing as simple as the unfolding of a given nature already in us at birth. Rather, they saw life on the analogy of self-expression in artistic creation. The creative artist does not express a meaning already present to him; but in creating the work of art he achieves a meaning that can then be seen as a completion or clarification of what had at first been sensed only incoherently. To see life as an analogous process in which education helps a person to make and clarify his nature may well improve on strict growth theories; but it re-emphasises that the educator himself cannot but choose what knowledge to make available to the learner as aids to self-expression and fulfilment.

(3) The idea of children choosing their own education does not really make sense. Choosing is not 'plumping for' or arbitrarily opting: it involves selecting on the basis of an informed understanding of available possibilities. One cannot make such informed selection unless one has already learned quite a lot about the possibilities. Choice cannot precede education, because choice presupposes a fair amount of education, formal or informal. However, this point does not rule out the possibility of a curriculum selected by teachers on the supposition that *ultimately* pupils will make their own choice of what is worthwhile. Accordingly, we can now consider J. P. White's contention that educators should abstain from making final judgements of worthwhileness and instead design a curriculum that will equip pupils to make such judgements.

J. P. White's Compulsory Curriculum

Paradoxically, White bases his argument for a compulsory curriculum (1973) on the fundamental moral principle of liberty. To prevent people doing what they want to do is wrong because it involves one person asserting his desires at the expense of another's. However, this principle can sometimes be over-ridden by other considerations: interference with some-one's liberty being justified to prevent his harming himself or others. So it would only be right to constrain a child to learn something if (1) he is likely to be harmed if he does not do so or (2) other people are likely to be harmed. Both possibilities are important but (1) is basic to White's case. But to know what it would be to harm a pupil we must ask what is the pupil's good. Intrinsic goods must be determined first, because things can only be extrinsic goods by leading on to intrinsic goods. White allows that it may be possible to develop a successful argument to show the intrinsic worth of activities, but believes that so far none has been achieved. This being so, it is morally wrong to teach on the supposition that certain curriculum activities must, for anyone, be superior to other pursuits. Indeed, it may be educationally damaging. For one who is taught to look on the pursuit of the arts or sciences for their own sake as a 'must' could be led to view them as moral 'musts'. This will make it difficult for him to see such pursuits as sources of personal satisfaction.

A very different approach is called for. Instead of asking what activities are worthwhile in themselves we should ask what activities are *educationally* worthwhile. We should look for reasons for teaching about activities without aspiring to find reasons for valuing them absolutely. To know what is good for pupils to learn we must have some notion of what is good for man. And since we can offer no objective account of what is good for *all* persons, we must say that what is intrinsically good for *a* man is what *he* would choose for its own sake. However, not *any* choosing would count here: choices based on momentary fancies or ignorance, or made in a disturbed state of mind, would not be satisfactory.

> In the ideal case what is wanted for its own sake on reflection is what a man would want for its own sake, given at least (a) that he knows of all other things which he might have preferred at that time and (b) that he has carefully considered priorities among these different choices, bearing in mind not only his present situation but also whether he is likely to alter his priorities in the future. (White, 1973, p. 20)

So, for a child about to be educated, we cannot know what the good for him will consist in. But we *can* know the position he must be in in order to determine his own good. He must be in, or as close as possible to, this ideal situation: 'He must know of all the possible things he may want to choose for their own sake, and he must be ready to consider what to choose from the point of view not only of the present moment but of his life as a whole' (ibid., p. 22). This being so, it would be actually harmful not to direct a child's education and to leave him ignorant of possibilities.

We must ensure (a) that he knows about as many activities or ways of life as possible which he may want to choose for their own sake, and (b) that he is able to reflect on priorities among them from the point of view not only of the present moment but as far as possible of his life as a whole. We are justified, therefore, in restricting his liberty as far as necessary to ensure (a) and (b): we are right to make him unfree now so as to give him as much autonomy as possible later on. (loc. cit.)

In this way White justifies a compulsory curriculum by reference to freedom, abdicating judgements of ultimate worth yet still making judgements of educational worth. In planning details of such a curriculum, he says, we must bear in mind that choices of activities do not stand alone: they are part of the choice of a way of life. Children must be educated to choose ways of life as well as activities. History, literature, biography and comparative religion and philosophy should be used to give students an informed vision of possible life-styles: the scholarly life, the sensuous life, the aesthetic life, the acquisitive life, the reforming life, and so on. (Typically, says White, schools do the opposite: encouraging pupils to think they are destined for one way of life and that other possibilities do not arise.)

Regarding knowledge of activities, White makes a distinction that has been the subject of some debate. Some activities which we may find intrinsically worthwhile need not be learned about because they come to us by nature: feeding, moving one's limbs, play, and so on. But other activities cannot be understood without learning. White divides these latter into Category

I activities where 'no understanding of what it is to want x is logically possible without engaging in x', and Category II activities where 'some understanding of what it is to want x is logically possible without engaging in x' (ibid., p. 26). An example of a Category I activity is linguistic communication, for 'one cannot understand at all what it is to communicate unless one can communicate'. Mountain-climbing, however, is a Category II activity, for 'One can understand *something* of what it is to climb mountains without having climbed one. A person who has never set foot on a mountain can understand something of what is going on in say, the film, *The Ascent of Everest*' (loc. cit.).

Category I activities include communication in general, engaging in pure mathematics and in the (exact) physical sciences, appreciating works of art, and philosophising.

Category II activities include speaking a foreign language, cricket, cookery and painting pictures (or writing poetry or composing music).

All children should study Category I activities as part of a compulsory curriculum. Such compulsion is justified on grounds of liberty because one who has not studied these subjects cannot know enough to make an informed choice whether to pursue them further. But there is no justification for compelling children to study Category II activities, for, without participating in them, children know enough to decide whether they want to participate in them. Such activities may have a place in schools but only as electives.

Thus White solves the practical problem which gave rise to questions of principle about the worthwhileness of activities: but he solves it by developing an argument from liberty which by-passes the question of ultimate worth. His solution is attractive in an important respect. It 'licenses' the teacher to teach the subject he cares for, untroubled by charges that he is imposing personal preferences on defenceless children. Even those who are not entirely happy with the argument may see it as the best working solution while the curriculum debate rages. However, some serious objections to the theory must be noted, though the idea that education should equip people to work out a life-style will be central to my argument in Chapter 3.

(1) It is doubtful whether Category I and Category II activi-

ties can be distinguished as crisply as White's case requires. It may not matter if there is minor disagreement with some details of the classification: minor changes in the lists would not be problematic. But it will be problematic if we doubt the validity of the distinction and conclude that informed judgements about any but the simplest of activities require participation. The Category I list would get very long and the curriculum-planner would have to do some selecting: presumably on grounds of worthwhileness! (White does consider these difficulties in his third chapter.)

(2) A possible objection to which White also attends is that of one who says that White is himself designing a curriculum to impose a subjective preference: the ideal of autonomy. He replies: 'I am not advocating any necessary commitment to an autonomous way of life. The child "must" become autonomous, to be sure, on the completion of his education . . . But whether the pupil then chooses to stay autonomous is up to him: if he becomes a slave or a "true believer" that is none of the teacher's business, at least, on the argument so far' (White, 1973, p. 23). A knowledge of Category I activities must be taught as the equipment to enable choice of activities and life-styles: and they can be forgotten once the choice is made.

But is White right here? Is it not the case that after an autonomous man has opted for an unreflective or heteronomous life he will always be aware of the possibility of returning to autonomy? Would not a decision not to return be itself an autonomous choice? White might have been on stronger ground had he argued that if liberty is a fundamental rational value then so must be autonomy.

(3) A related point is that if we have been taught about and participated in a Category I activity to the point where we can claim to know what it involves, then it is doubtful whether we can just set that activity aside and bother with it no more. Does not coming to understand any serious activity involve coming to feel something of its 'call' or 'urgency'? Would we not be sceptical of one who said 'Oh, I know what there is in that poetry business (or science, or history, or music): I think I'll give it a miss'? Certainly it would be odd if someone said 'In my early twenties I *decided* to be interested in philosophy'? For people just do not relate to serious activities in this way. Many

philosophers have a love-hate relationship with their subject. They would like to have fun or do good works; but, having learned to see what there is in philosophical problems, they do not feel free simply to set them aside.

(4) This suggests fears that White's approach might have educationally unfortunate consequences he could hardly wish for. It is generally thought that a good teacher must care passionately for his subject, evidencing this passion and getting pupils to share it. But who could sustain such passion if he saw himself as merely offering a *smörgåsbrod* of pursuits to be sampled and then freely chosen or rejected? Does not good teaching presuppose a more positive conviction of the worth of what we teach? In Chapter 3 I try to argue grounds for such conviction that are compatible with a high regard for freedom.

3

Towards a Positive Answer

In Chapter 1 I distinguished knowledge that earns a place in the curriculum because it is thought useful, from knowledge that is valued and also seems to belong in the curriculum regardless of usefulness. This second kind of knowledge, it was suggested, must therefore have value as a good or end in itself. The problem then was to show (1) why we are justified in regarding such knowledge as intrinsically good, and (2) how such knowledge is to be recognised. In Chapter 2 we surveyed possible answers to these questions and found serious difficulties with all of them. If, then, we have reached an unsatisfactory position, this may be because of something wrong with the initial presentation of the problem. And it will now be argued that the mistake is to accept the long-established dichotomy between knowledge as a means to an end and knowledge as an end in itself. The argument will be in three stages.

Stage (1)   The notion of knowledge as an end in itself is unsatisfactory.

Stage (2)   The dichotomy overlooks a third possibility: that some knowledge is valuable neither as a means to an end, nor as an end in itself, but because it helps us to determine our ends.

Stage (3)   This view has radical implications for the curriculum.

(1) It will be argued that the notion of knowledge as an end in itself is seriously ambiguous, and that if we overcome the

ambiguity with crisper specifications it becomes highly untenable: but untenable for reasons that point towards the third possibility, just mentioned. When people talk of knowledge as an end in itself it is simply not clear what is being canvassed. They could mean that the mere fact of someone having the knowledge is a good, or that satisfactions associated with the pursuit and achievement of knowledge are good. Strictly speaking, the latter view does not value knowledge as an end in itself, but values the pursuit and achievement of knowledge for its psychological by-products.

A further ambiguity is between the idea that it is intrinsically good for any individual person to possess knowledge, and that it is intrinsically good for the sum total of human knowledge to exist and grow. The first notion would be appropriate to justifying a non-useful curriculum: the second to justifying non-useful research. Peters notes an unfortunate consequence of overlooking this ambiguity (1977a, p. 56). University professors, enthusiastic for their specialised research, may want to share this enthusiasm by lecturing about their speciality to undergraduates seeking a 'general' education. The professor may justify his course by reference to knowledge as an end in itself. But what he finds intrinsically valuable as an addition to the corpus of human knowledge may not impress the student: the student may only recognise knowledge as a good in itself if it strikes him as the sort of thing everyone ought to study. Thus teacher and learner think of themselves as engaged in the common pursuit of knowledge for its own sake when really they are at cross-purposes. The consequence is student dissatisfaction and complaints of irrelevancy.

A third ambiguity is less obvious. Advocates of a liberal education into the various areas of knowledge often argue the value of this by reference to the qualities of mind that such studies nurture. Thus it is said that the study of poetry develops our power to make fine discriminations of meaning; that science teaches careful observation; that philosophy nurtures rigorous thinking; that history broadens our vision by liberating us from temporal parochialism. Commonly it is held that such studies will only have this mind-improving effect if we pursue them disinterestedly. Thus we get admittedly paradoxical suggestions that, say, we must become absorbed in philosophy entirely for its own sake if we are to acquire those powers of rigorous, impartial thinking that are valuable in real life.

Now this sounds like a clear case of an argument from usefulness: the value of the disinterested study consisting in the useful powers of mind it will nurture (which is why it has not been considered so far in this book). However, it is not quite so clear-cut: for it can be argued that the qualities of mind associated with the various areas of knowledge are inseparable from, and constitutive of, those areas of knowledge. For example, to be able to engage in a particular style of rigorous argument *is* to be able to do philosophy; an awareness of certain kinds of subtlety of meaning *is* a poetic awareness; to be liberated from temporal parochialism *is* to acquire historical perspective. Writers like Newman and Arnold were surely right to insist that it is not enough to be educated into the various areas of human knowledge and achievement, to insist that one must study the best that there is in these areas. For the best philosophical rigour only exists in the best philosophy: the finest poetic sensibility only exists in the best poetry. It seems that we cannot really separate out from the study of a subject the qualities of mind generated by such study: the distinction between extrinsic and intrinsic worth breaks down.

A like point emerges if we approach the question from another angle and ask what sense we can make of the idea of studying philosophy as a completely disinterested pursuit quite unrelated to how we think about our lives, or of the study of science as having nothing to do with how we see the physical world.

Peters also notes another ambiguity (1977a, pp. 51–2). If someone studies anatomy because he wants to relieve suffering we might incline to say that he is pursuing this knowledge as a means to a further practical end. Yet, contrasting him with one who studies anatomy to gain wealth and status, we might say he was interested in his subject for its own sake. Peters concludes that the dichotomy between 'knowledge for its own sake' and 'knowledge for particular ends' is too coarse to discriminate the different ways in which knowledge can be pursued for ends related to, but distinct from, that knowledge. Shortly I shall argue that acceptance of this oversimple dichotomy has caused us to overlook a hugely important way in which knowledge is valuable.

Meanwhile, faced with such ambiguities, we might try to tighten up the notion of knowledge as a good in itself, saying that the notion refers either to the bare fact of knowledge being acquired, or (less tightly) to the satisfaction associated with the pursuit and acquisition of knowledge. Regarding the second and looser interpretation it can hardly be doubted that the pursuit and attainment of knowledge seems to be a widespread source of satisfaction. To this extent at least the pursuit and enjoyment of knowledge must earn a place in the range of possible goods: particularly so if we follow those theorists discussed in Chapter 2 who hold that man naturally desires to know. But this is hardly adequate as a theory of curriculum justification, as we saw in the discussion of naturalistic justification in Chapter 2. Furthermore, as Augustine believed, charges of indulgence can be brought against a curriculum that simply satisfies human curiosity rather than equips the learner to attend to more over-riding obligations.

Difficulties also arise with the tighter interpretation, whereby the bare fact of someone's possessing knowledge is regarded as intrinsically good. We have already seen how hard it is to answer one who just does not see why we should set value on the mere fact of knowing. A further difficulty is important because it points towards the more positive case to be developed shortly: it is that anyone who says knowledge is an end in itself is unlikely to claim that all knowledge is equally of such intrinsic value. It would seem absurd to claim intrinsic value for totally trivial knowledge. Can anyone believe that there could be even the slightest intrinsic value in my suddenly coming to know the product of the number of letters on this page multiplied by the number of sparrows breeding in Hyde Park last March? Could we seriously say that not to know this is to be in an inferior state?

But this reduction to absurdity yields a positive clue. For advocates of knowledge as intrinsically valuable seem to have in mind no such bizarre snippets of pointless data, but organised bodies of knowledge that could reasonably be described as 'serious' or 'significant'. They might allow the absurdity of my examples yet claim intrinsic worth for a knowledge of the structure of the Milky Way, of early hominoid remains in Africa or of Christian symbolism in Renaissance art. But such claims presuppose some standard or criterion of significance and seriousness, even if this has not been made explicit. And it is hard to see why we should regard knowledge as 'significant' or 'serious' for any reason other than the fact that it can fuse with other knowledge to become part of the overall view a man takes of the world he inhabits and of himself in that world. In his daily living a man may be unlikely to *use* knowledge about his early ancestors, the size of the universe, or the meaning of great art. Yet such knowledge can still be important to his life: important not as inert knowledge unrelated to how he lives and merely contemplated for its own sake; rather, it is knowledge that helps to shape a man's view of things in general so as to become part of the very texture of how he understands and lives his life. Such areas of knowledge are significant and valuable to a man because they can become part of his 'world view' or 'philosophy of life'. They are valuable to him neither as a means to an end nor as an end in themselves. We see more fully how this is so in the next stage of the argument.

(2) It is reasonable, then, to attribute inherent worth not to all or any knowledge, but only to bodies of serious or significant knowledge. But this seriousness or significance puts such knowledge into a third value category. It is not valuable as an end in itself, for it is serious or significant in so far as it makes a difference to how one lives. But neither is it useful, for it is not knowledge that is to be used to some further end. Rather, it is the kind of knowledge that helps us to determine our ends. By this I mean that it gives us that picture or understanding of things in terms of which we can decide what to do with our lives, what aims to set ourselves, what ends to live for.

Thus it seems that when people find bodies of knowledge significant and valuable, even though they are likely to be of little or no use, then talk of such knowledge as a good or end in itself is unfortunate. The motive for such talk is the appropriate one of denying any practical interest in the use that might be made of such knowledge; but this way of putting it misleadingly suggests knowledge that is valued quite apart from any bearing it has on our lives. Such knowledge is valuable just because it is important to our lives, though not because it is useful.

As this point is the nub of my argument I will attempt

elucidation by approaching it from a different perspective: by approaching it through questions people often ask about 'the meaning of life'. Laymen often ask philosophers to tell them 'the meaning of life' and are taken aback when they get unhelpful or dismissive answers. Philosophers may give such answers because they have in mind the rather pedantic point that strictly speaking the request is unanswerable since life does not have meaning in the way that signs, symbols, gestures and words have meanings. Or, less offensively, they may have in mind that questions about the meaning of life really run together a complex mixture of questions about why the world is as it is, how we should live, whether there is a plan behind the universe, and so on. They probably think that everyone should do his own puzzling over these questions rather than ask philosophers to dispense instant answers.

Now, people wonder about the 'meaning of life' when they are not just puzzled about how they should live and about the point of their lives, but are puzzled over such questions in a way that relates them to other very general puzzles about ourselves and our world. Questions about how we should live become linked to questions about how or why we come to be here, why we are as we are, and why the world is as it is. Clearly, such questions cannot be briefly answered: they only become manageable by being broken down. The various questions involved must be discriminated for separate consideration without overlooking interrelations. Such articulation will yield more or less straightforwardly empirical questions about the nature of ourselves and of our physical and social environments, theological questions as to whether we and our universe are accidental occurrences or belong to some overall plan, and value questions about right conduct and what is worth living for. Accordingly, reflection on 'the meaning of life' is bound to be an extraordinarily complex business involving all the great fields of human knowledge: natural science, human science, morality, history, theology, aesthetics, and so on. Such knowledge then becomes non-useful yet valuable other than as an end in itself: valuable because it throws light on fundamental puzzles that lie behind talk about 'the meaning of life'. Since these puzzles arise from, and are focused on, questions about what ends we should pursue, then knowledge that helps us to reflect on them helps us to form a 'world view' and determine our ends. Such knowledge is valuable in a way that we overlook if we accept as exhaustive the dichotomy between knowledge as a means to an end and knowledge as an end in itself.

This view of how some knowledge is supremely valuable to human beings seems to justify a curriculum that aspires to educate everyone into 'culture' or 'the higher learning'. Shortly I shall spell out more precise educational applications of these very general notions. First, however, this theory of curriculum justification must be strengthened by reference to a view of human nature: a view of human nature often associated with, though not the monopoly of, existentialist philosophers. To do this may seem to contradict what was said in Chapter 2 regarding the difficulty of squaring any theory of human nature with the diversity of human life-styles, values and aspirations. But this variability of human nature can be taken as testifying both to the fact of human freedom (in the sense that what we do and become is not just causally predetermined but is also a matter of free choice) and also to the fact that we exercise this freedom through a socially inherited body of ideas and institutions. For it is through this cultural inheritance that we learn to see possibilities for the exercise of our freedom. Thinkers sometimes make these points with remarks like 'It is man's nature not to have a nature', or 'Man has no nature: he has a history'. Such a view of the indeterminateness of human nature can point to what is appropriate for us to study and learn by virtue of our humanity: though not after the manner of the naturalistic theories discussed earlier. Rather, my argument is that to be human is to act freely in the world, though within the constraints that the world imposes; and that to act freely is not just to do something, but to do it with at least some notion of and about what one is doing. This being so, our free actions in the world necessarily presuppose some body of ideas about ourselves and our world. Since such ideas can hardly be generated by each of us individually, they must be socially inherited through processes of formal and informal education. In other words, it is impossible for us to conduct ourselves as humans except in so far as we have had passed on to us some sort of culture; some body of ideas about ourselves, our world and our fellows, about how we are to conduct ourselves towards that world and those fellows, about what ends we might set ourselves in life.

Given this, it must surely follow that we should educate human beings into such a cultural inheritance as will best fit them for the distinctively human enterprise of working out what sorts of human beings they are to make of themselves. To say this presupposes that we can evaluate a possible cultural inheritance: and this we can do, though it is very difficult. For an inheritance may carry a picture of the world that is accurate or distorting, informed or ignorant. It may guide us to better or worse moralities. It may open up to us rich possibilities for conceiving the world and conducting our lives, or render us blind or hostile towards whole realms of human awareness and endeavour. The concern of education should be, in the light of such considerations, to discern and pass on the best culture possible.

If this argument is correct, then some of the criticisms made of Hirst's theory in Chapter 2 will now be seen to be extremely important. For there it was argued that Hirst's concern that pupils master the distinctive logics of the various forms of knowledge invites inattention to questions about what content is important. The subject matter of knowledge does much more than the 'logic' to inform the way a man views his life and its possibilities, so it must be centrally important to ask what bodies of knowledge and ideas are most valuable in this regard; though of course the 'logic' of the forms needs to be mastered to enable one to grasp such knowledge.

It might be doubted whether all this really makes the case I want it to make. For if it is true that a human being growing up in society will inherit a culture which gives him *a* way of seeing himself and his circumstance, then it still has to be shown why we should take the trouble to initiate people into the less easily acquired culture embodied in intellectual disciplines. As we saw in Chapter 2, Elliott raises the possibility that the disciplines do not afford anyone an understanding of things superior to that offered by the common understanding that we acquire effortlessly. But while it is therefore important that educational philosophers engage in critical scrutiny of the disciplines, there are grounds for believing that in general the disciplines do have important virtues. Thus, when a discipline flourishes, competition between scholars and doctrines ensures constant scrutiny, criticism, correction and refinement of thought. Further, the disciplines persist and grow through generations, epochs, and even cultures: they are thereby partially protected against parochialism and can embody accumulated ideas and insights from those who have viewed a subject from widely different perspectives. Accordingly, a world view informed by the disciplines is likely to be more rigorous and self-critical, less parochial, and much enriched from the achievements of many thinkers.

To summarise, then, it has been argued that we are right to believe that the great, evolved bodies of knowledge and speculation have a value and educational importance that is independent of, and greater than, the value of usefulness. But it is wrong to conclude that their value must therefore be as ends in themselves. Rather they are of value because they help us in the inescapably human enterprise of forming a 'world view' or 'philosophy of life' whereby we set ourselves ends in life. They help us to reflect on the kinds of questions that are involved in puzzles about 'the meaning of life'. Thus a body of knowledge earns a place in the curriculum on grounds other than usefulness if, and in so far as, it is likely to contribute to the working out of such a world view. These conclusions may gain clarity as we consider just some of their practical applications.

(3) If we now relate the view just argued to practical educational planning, the main areas of knowledge appropriate to the education of human beings as human beings appear to be the following.

(a) Perhaps the most obviously important are the natural sciences, with the support of mathematics. These offer us a view of the nature, composition, extent and origin of our physical circumstance and of our own physical make-up. Here, of course, what matters is the natural sciences in their 'cosmological' aspect rather than a series of discrete topics unrelated to any overall view of things.

(b) Historical studies are important to place our circumstance and culture in a temporal perspective, showing its past growth and origins and perhaps pointing to future developments. At the same time history reveals to us the limitations and contingency of our present modes of thinking. By juxtaposing other ages and cultures it warns us against the human tendency to regard the present as the universal norm, and alerts us to the richness of human possibilities.

(c) History also belongs with the 'behavioural sciences' and with much literature as the study of persons. Disciplines with different logics and procedures all seek a better understanding of ourselves and our fellows.

(d) Religious studies are central. To explore mankind's religions is to explore the various attempts to fathom the divine and to discern any ultimate purpose behind the cosmos and our lives.

(e) All these areas of inquiry interact and mutually inform one another. At the same time their claims and pretensions are open to question. Here philosophy is doubly important, helping us both to synthesise disparate disciplines into a coherent world view, and to scrutinise the foundations and validity of these disciplines along the lines already suggested.

(f) Since an education into culture as here understood is to do with action as well as understanding (all these areas of study being important to the formation of a world view that will inform the way we live our lives), then such education must have a central moral and practical dimension. The various areas outlined must be related both to an understanding of right and wrong and to all practical deliberations.

(g) The place of the arts in the kind of curriculum here advocated is less easy to determine. This will seem paradoxical following much talk of an education into culture; for the realm of the arts is often regarded as, supremely, the cultural realm. The difficulty arises out of differing views on the nature of the arts. If we agree with those who believe that all the arts attempt to understand the world, then there is no doubting their importance according to the theory here proposed. But if we agree with those who assign the aesthetic to an autonomous world of the imagination cut off from life and reality, then it becomes harder to determine its place in education. We might say that in the arts we have a body of human achievements that men have found valuable not just to embellish their lives, but to become the object of their best endeavours. It would be an incomplete education into what we might make of our lives that did not include this dimension. That there are such difficulties nicely illustrates why reflection on the nature and point of all areas of knowledge should be a main concern of curriculum theorists.

The argument so far may seem to endorse a typical traditional curriculum. That this is far from the case becomes evident when we work out details. For in teaching any of the areas outlined the guiding intention will be to teach that area in such a way that it helps people to work out a 'world view' or 'philosophy of life'. I will take the teaching of natural science as an example. It will, of course, be important to teach something of the logical and procedural bases of the sciences: for without this scientific propositions are not really understood, their fallibility is not appreciated, and they cannot be seen as part of a continuing adventure of inquiry. However, the aim will not be to train scientific researchers. Centrally important will be something that in fact is rarely attempted either for the apprentice research worker or for the study of science as a 'general' or 'liberal' study; that is, to present an overall view of the achievements of science in the attempt to explain the mysteries of our physical environment. Contemporary scientists are making startling researches into such matters as the origin of life, the evolution of man, the age and dimension of the universe, the physical basis of mind and the nature of matter. Their findings are potentially important to the view that we form of our world and ourselves, and this earns them a place in a curriculum appropriate to human beings. Yet today even the best-educated layman is likely to be little informed on these researches. We can understand why this is so. There was a time when men who made scientific advances could write about them in works that would be widely read and understood by anyone who had been reasonably schooled. But in order to progress, science has had to become technical and specialised. Typically, researchers now push ahead with discrete inquiries which cannot be widely understood and which are never synthesised into a growing picture of the natural order. Almost inevitably, science has thus lost sight of its original and splendid purpose of seeking a better understanding of the world we live in. To retrieve the situation is an immensely difficult task for science education. Much work will have to be done devising ways to teach the findings of science in their cosmological aspects to those who do not have the technical knowledge of specialist researchers; care being taken to ensure that difficult subject matter is rendered readily comprehensible without being distorted or debased.

Similar reforms are implied in the teaching of other subjects, and I hope that readers will feel encouraged to work out what these might be in their own specialist areas. Clearly, the sort of reforms being proposed will not be easy, especially as we must leave room to teach all those useful things which are also important in education. Such reforms might prove impossibly difficult; in which case, there can be no teaching of the kind of curriculum proposed here as appropriate to human beings. But the argument has shown, I hope, that we ought to *try* to teach such a curriculum: for it is a curriculum demanded by the nature of man as a free being who must form a world view and decide what to make of himself and his life. Educators who are diffident about doing this risk neglecting to pass on to their pupils the knowledge and ideas that will equip them to make the best possible sense of their lives. And pupils who are not educated to inform their lives with the best in our cultural inheritance will be left, as indeed they often are, to rely on the ephemeral, the homespun and the third-rate.

To conclude, I must answer two possible criticisms of the case I have proposed. The argument of this chapter could be summarised by saying that we should try to teach to everyone the knowledge that helps us to think about the kinds of question we often express by asking about 'the meaning of life'. It might be said that there is something selfishly indulgent about this, that such a curriculum would encourage a pupil to be concerned with his own life to the neglect of moral obligations. However, I have taken 'meaning of life' questions to include questions about our moral obligations and how we are to act on them. It might also be protested that 'meaning of life' questions are never likely to be finally answered, so that to pursue them is to court frustration and despair. Certainly if human beings join, in a spirit of mutual respect and co-operation, in the attempt to fathom life's mysteries, then they are unlikely ever to *discover* the meaning of life. They may, however, find that by seriously engaging in such inquiries they have put meaning into their lives.

4

Suggestions for Further Reading

Generally I have given references to appropriate texts in the course of discussing various doctrines. In most cases these will give the best leads for readers wishing to look more fully into any particular viewpoint. There are, however, further texts to be recommended regarding some of the theorists. I shall mention these before going on to suggestions that will help readers pursue three central themes in the book.

Regarding any particular thinker or doctrine, reference to *The Encyclopedia of Philosophy* (Edwards, 1967) is likely to be rewarding. Aristotle's philosophy as a whole is outlined in G. E. R. Lloyd's *Aristotle: The Growth and Structure of his Thought* (1968) and there is a good discussion of his educational doctrines in W. K. Frankenna's *Three Historical Philosophies of Education* (1965). G. Howie has edited and introduced a selection, *Aristotle on Education* (1968). A. Quinton's *Utilitarian Ethics* (1973) is one of several good general accounts of this school of moral philosophy, and includes references to modern discussions. W. H. Burston has edited James Mill's educational writings, *James Mill on Education* (1969). Frankenna (op. cit.) has a most valuable discussion of Dewey, and M. Skilbeck has edited and introduced a selection of Dewey's own educational writings, *John Dewey* (1970). Peters has edited a collection of critical papers of varying quality, *John Dewey Reconsidered* (1977b). The aspect of Kant's philosophy that was discussed in the 'Man as striver' section in Chapter 2 is excitingly presented

94

in Cassirer's *Rousseau, Kant and Goethe* (1945) which is also excellent background reading to the child-centred protest. The many general introductions to Plato include G. C. Field's *The Philosophy of Plato* (1969), while the motivation for Plato's theory of forms is clearly explained in Gilbert Ryle's entry on Plato in *The Encyclopedia of Philosophy* (Edwards, 1967). R. Nettleship's classic study *The Theory of Education in Plato's Republic* (1935) does not include a great deal that is pertinent to our present theme. Careful discussion of the epistemological aspects of Hirst's theory of the curriculum can be found in two journal articles by D. C. Phillips (1971) and E. Hindess (1972). There is also a useful if irritatingly arrogant discussion in Chapter III of Warnock's *Schools of Thought* (1977). Hirst acknowledges his debt to the epistemological work of D. W. Hamlyn, much of which is summarised in Hamlyn's *Theory of Knowledge* (1971). Apart from the texts discussed, R. S. Peters has written three further papers on our topic. 'Subjectivity and standards' is included in his collection *Psychology and Ethical Development* (1974) and his *Education and the Education of Teachers* (1977a) contains two illuminating papers on the concept of liberal education. Howie has edited a collection *St Augustine on Education* (1969b) which can be usefully studied in conjunction with his monograph (1969a). Emotivist theories of value have been an important focus of modern philosophical debate and there is much literature on the subject. A useful introduction to the several versions of the doctrine is Brandt's 'Emotive theory of ethics' in *The Encyclopedia of Philosophy* (Edwards, 1967). Any work on the history of educational ideas will discuss at least some of the child-centred reformers discussed in Chapter 2: but too often the tendency is to summarise educational recommendations without relating these to the underlying views of man, society, knowledge and values. L. Claydon has edited and introduced a selection of Rousseau's educational writings, *Rousseau on Education* (1969), and there is a helpful paper by J. Plamenatz (1972). Notwithstanding the reforms initiated in Froebel's name, there seems to have been no adequate attempt to get to the heart of his vision. R. F. Dearden (1972) has subjected growth theories to powerful criticism. Selections from A. S. Neill's many writings are conveniently brought together in *Summerhill* (1968) and the reader will understand why it is so difficult to feel confident that one has represented Neill's views accurately. Probably the best book about Neill is R. Hemmings's *Fifty Years of Freedom* (1972) and there is also a good discussion in R. Skidelsky's *English Progressive Schools* (1969). More recent works arguing for pupil choice of curriculum are I. Illich's *De-Schooling Society* (1971) and E. Reimer's *School Is Dead* (1971). This whole tradition is subjected to lively and informed criticism in R. Barrow's *Radical Education* (1978). The positive case that I have tried to develop in Chapter 3 is greatly indebted to J. Ortega y Gasset's readable *Mission of the University* (1946).

Three themes are central to the problem as I have presented it: (1) values, (2) human nature and (3) evaluation of the disciplines. All three offer infinite scope for further reading and reflection and I can only suggest what seem to me to promise to be helpful leads.

(1) Values

Most philosophical discussions of values have been about moral values. This is generally appropriate, if unfortunate from the perspective of our present concerns. The best initial approach is probably through a good introductory text in ethics. Apart from works already mentioned the following, all with different approaches, can be recommended: K. Baier's *The Moral Point of View* (1958), J. Hospers's *Human Conduct* (1964), W. D. Hudson's *Modern Moral Philosophy* (1970) and A. MacIntyre's *A Short History of Ethics* (1966). Doubts about the crispness of the fact-value distinction are explored in a collection of papers on *The Is-Ought Question* edited by W. D. Hudson (1969).

(2) Human Nature

Stuart Hampshire's difficult and important *Thought and Action* (1959) develops the kind of view of human nature that is presupposed in Chapter 3 of this book. Mary Midgley's *Beast and Man* (1978) looks critically at some modern views of human nature derived from recent developments in science. E.

Cassirer's *An Essay on Man* (1945) has become a classic and is rich in educational interest. D. I. Lloyd has a short essay, 'Nature of man', in *Philosophy and the Teacher* (1976). Isaiah Berlin's *Vico and Herder* (1976) discusses two somewhat neglected thinkers who are historically important for having drawn attention to the ways in which man's 'nature' varies between epochs and cultures.

(3) Evaluation of the Disciplines

In Chapter 3 I argued that it is important that educational philosophers should look critically at the established disciplines of learning. A first move in this direction would be to study philosophical works which seek to elucidate the nature and rational basis of the various forms of knowledge. The abundance of such literature includes S. Toulmin's *The Philosophy of Science* (1953) and A. F. Chalmers's *What Is This Thing Called Science?* (1976) which covers the lively debates that have taken place in this area since 1953. Peter Winch's exciting and controversial *The Idea of a Social Science* (1958) maintains that the human sciences *must* be very different from the natural sciences. Richard Wolheim's *Art and its Objects* (1970) is difficult but rewarding. W. H. Dray's *Philosophy of History* (1964), J. Hick's *Philosophy of Religion* (1973) and S. Körner's *The Philosophy of Mathematics* (1960) can all be recommended. All these works give good leads to other writings in the area. However, they are only starting points for the kind of critique of the disciplines I have proposed: a critique which attends not only to the validity of the various disciplines as they now exist, but also to how the disciplines can enter into and transform a man's view of himself and his world. There can be no short cut to such a critique: one must study the discipline as it is developing and as it is entering into human lives. To this end one must read far and wide, attending to the literature of the discipline itself and perhaps also learning from the reflections and autobiographies of those who have worked in it. It is also important to acquire historical perspective and explore ways in which disciplines have changed as their role in human culture has changed. P. Gardiner's extensive collection of readings, *The*

Philosophy of History (1974), will help one to do this for just one discipline. Even more pertinent are those historical studies which also attend to the impact a discipline has had on other areas of human life and understanding; an excellent example is Morris Klein's *Mathematics in Western Culture* (1972) and three companion works by S. Toulmin and J. Goodfield: *The Fabric of the Heavens* (1961), *The Architecture of Matter* (1962) and *The Discovery of Time* (1965). The importance of criticism of the various disciplines will be evident from the use I have made of Passmore's *Science and its Critics* (1978). More radical criticisms of the way science is presently understood and conducted (though not of science as such) are P. K. Feyerabend's *Against Method* (1975) and N. Maxwell's *What's Wrong with Science?* (1976). Edmund Husserl's understanding of post-Galilean physics is explained in A. Gurwitsch's 'Galilean physics in the light of Husserl's phenomenology' (1978).

But it must be stressed once more: these are only starting suggestions for what is, if my argument has been correct, a rich and important area for development in philosophy of education.

References

al-Attas, S. M. al-N. (ed.) (1979), *Aims and Objectives of Muslim Education* (Sevenoaks, Kent: Hodder & Stoughton).

Aristotle (1953), *The Nicomachean Ethics*, trans. J. A. K. Thompson as *The Ethics of Aristotle* (London: Allen & Unwin). I have used the original page references; these are given in most editions, including that listed here.

Augustine, St (1979), *Confessions*, trans. R. S. Pine-Coffin (Harmondsworth, Mddx: Penguin).

Ayer, A. J. (1971), *Language, Truth and Logic* [1936] (Harmondsworth, Middx: Penguin).

Baier, K. (1958), *The Moral Point of View* (Ithaca, NY: Cornell University Press).

Barrow, R. (1976), *Common Sense and the Curriculum* (London: Allen & Unwin).

Barrow, R. (1978), *Radical Education* (London: Martin Robertson).

Bell, C. (1914), *Art* (London: Chatto & Windus).

Bentham, J. (1907), *An Introduction to the Principles of Morals and Legislation* [1823] (Oxford: Clarendon Press).

Berlin, I. (1976), *Vico and Herder* (London: Hogarth Press).

Blanshard, B. (1973), *The Uses of a Liberal Education and Other Talks to Students* (La Salle, Ill.: Open Court).

Brandt, R. B. (1967), 'Emotive theory of ethics', in Edwards (1967), Vol. 2, pp. 493–6.

Burston, W. H. (ed.) (1969), *James Mill on Education* (Cambridge: CUP).

Cassirer, E. (1945a), *An Essay on Man* (New Haven, Conn.: Yale University Press).

Cassirer, E. (1945b), *Rousseau, Kant and Goethe*, trans. J. Gutmann, P. K. Kristeller and J. H. Randall (Princeton, NJ: Princeton University Press).

Chalmers, A. F. (1976), *What Is This Thing Called Science?* (St Lucia, Queensland: University of Queensland Press).

Claydon, L. (ed.) (1969), *Rousseau on Education* (London: Collier Macmillan).

Dearden, R. F. (1972), 'Education as a process of growth', in R. F. Dearden, P. H. Hirst and R. S. Peters (eds), *Education and the Development of Reason* (London: Routledge & Kegan Paul), pp. 65–84.

Dewey, J. (1963), *Experience and Education* [1938] (London: Collier Macmillan).

Dray, W. H. (1964), *Philosophy of History* (Englewood Cliffs, NJ: Prentice-Hall).

Edwards, P. (ed.) (1967), *The Encyclopedia of Philosophy* (New York: Macmillan/The Free Press).

Elliott, R. K. (1975), 'Education and human being', in S. C. Brown (ed.), *Philosophers Discuss Education* (London: Macmillan), pp. 45–72.

Elliott, R. K. (1977), 'Education and justification', *Proceedings of the Philosophy of Education Society of Great Britain*, vol XI, pp. 7–27.

Feyerabend, P. K. (1975), *Against Method* (London: New Left Books).

Field, G. C. (1969), *The Philosophy of Plato* [1949], 2nd edn (London: OUP).

Frankenna, W. K. (1965), *Three Historical Philosophies of Education* (Chicago: Scott, Foresman).

Gardiner, P. (ed.) (1974), *The Philosophy of History* (London: OUP).

Gurwitsch, A. (1978), 'Galilean physics in the light of Husserl's phenomenology', in T. Luckman (ed.), *Phenomenology and Sociology* (Harmondsworth, Mddx: Penguin), pp. 71–89.

Hamlyn, D. W. (1971), *Theory of Knowledge* (London: Macmillan).

Hampshire, S. (1959), *Thought and Action* (London: Chatto & Windus).

Hardie, C. D. (1962), *Truth and Fallacy in Educational Theory* [1942] (Columbia, NY: Teachers College, Columbia University).

Hemmings, R. (1972), *Fifty Years of Freedom* (London: Allen & Unwin).

Hick, J. (1973), *Philosophy of Religion* [1963], 2nd edn (Englewood Cliffs, NJ: Prentice-Hall).

Hindess, E. (1972), 'Forms of knowledge', *Proceedings of the Philosophy of Education Society of Great Britain*, vol. VI, no. 2, pp. 164–75.

Hirst, P. H. (1974), *Knowledge and the Curriculum* (London: Routledge & Kegan Paul).

Hirst, P. H., and Peters, R. S. (1970), *The Logic of Education* (London: Routledge & Kegan Paul).

Holmes, E. (1911), *What Is and What Might Be* (London: Constable).

Hospers, J. (1964), *Human Conduct* (New York: Harcourt, Brace & World).

Howie, G. (ed.) (1968), *Aristotle on Education* (London: Collier Macmillan).

Howie, G. (1969a), *Educational Theory and Practice in St Augustine* (London: Routledge & Kegan Paul).

Howie, G. (ed.) (1969b), *St Augustine on Education* (South Bend, Ind.: Gateway).

Hudson, W. D. (ed.) (1969), *The Is-Ought Question* (London: Macmillan).

Hudson, W. D. (1970), *Modern Moral Philosophy* (London: Macmillan).

Illich, I. (1971), *De-Schooling Society* (Harmondsworth, Mddx: Penguin).

Kant, I. (1914), *Critique of Judgment* [1790], 2nd edn, trans. J. H. Bernard (London: Macmillan).

Klein, M. (1972), *Mathematics in Western Culture* (Harmondsworth, Mddx: Penguin).

Körner, S. (1960), *The Philosophy of Mathematics* (London: Hutchinson).

Lilley, I. M. (ed.) (1967), *Friedrich Froebel: A Selection from his Writings* (Cambridge: CUP).

Lloyd, D. I. (ed.) (1976), 'Nature of man', in D. I. Lloyd, *Philosophy and the Teacher* (London: Routledge & Kegan Paul), pp. 31–40.

Lloyd, G. E. R. (1968), *Aristotle: The Growth and Structure of his Thought* (Cambridge: CUP).

REFERENCES

MacIntyre, A. C. (1964), 'Against utilitarianism', in T. H. B. Hollins (ed.), *Aims in Education: The Philosophical Approach* (Manchester: Manchester University Press), pp. 1–23.

MacIntyre, A. C. (1966), *A Short History of Ethics* (New York: Macmillan).

Mark, K. (1930), *Capital* [1893] (London: Dent).

Maxwell, N. (1976), *What's Wrong with Science?* (Frome, Somerset: Bran's Head Books).

Midgley, M. (1978), *Beast and Man* (Hassocks, Sussex: Harvester Press).

Mill, J. S. (1910), *Utilitarianism, Liberty and Representative Government* [1863] (London: Dent).

Moore, G. E. (1960), *Principia Ethica* [1903] (Cambridge: CUP).

Neill, A. S. (1968), *Summerhill* (Harmondsworth, Mddx: Penguin).

Nettleship, R. (1935), *The Theory of Education in Plato's Republic* (Oxford: Clarendon Press).

Newman, J. H. (1915), *On the Scope and Nature of University Education* [1852] (London: Dent).

Newsom, J. (1963), *Half Our Future: Report of the Central Advisory Council for Education (England)* (London: HMSO).

O'Connor, D. J. (1957), *An Introduction to the Philosophy of Education* (London: Routledge & Kegan Paul).

Ortega y Gasset, J. (1946), *Mission of the University*, trans. H. L. Nostrand (London: Kegan Paul, Trench & Trubner).

Passmore, J. (1978), *Science and its Critics* (London: Duckworth).

Pater, W. (1961), *The Renaissance: Studies in Art and Poetry* [1873] (London: Collins/Fontana).

Paterson, R. K. W. (1979), 'Towards an axiology of knowledge', *Journal of Philosophy of Education*, vol. 13, pp. 91–100.

Peters, R. S. (1966), *Ethics and Education* (London: Allen & Unwin).

Peters, R. S. (1973), 'The justification of education', in R. S. Peters (ed.), *The Philosophy of Education* (London: OUP), pp. 239–67.

Peters, R. S. (1974), *Psychology and Ethical Development* (London: Allen & Unwin).

Peters, R. S. (1977a), *Education and the Education of Teachers* (London: Routledge & Kegan Paul).

Peters, R. S. (ed.) (1977b), *John Dewey Reconsidered* (London: Routledge & Kegan Paul).

Phillips, D. C. (1971), 'The distinguishing features of forms of knowledge', *Educational Philosophy and Theory*, vol. 3, no. 2, pp. 27–35.

Plamenatz, J. (1972), 'Rousseau: the education of Emile', in *Proceedings of the Philosophy of Education Society of Great Britain*, vol. VI, no. 2, pp. 176–92.

Plato, *The Republic*. Quotations are from H. D. P. Lee's translation (Harmondsworth, Mddx: Penguin, 1955) but I have used the original pagination which is included in this edition, for references.

Quinton, A. (1973), *Utilitarian Ethics* (London: Macmillan).

Reimer, E. (1971), *School Is Dead* (Harmondsworth, Mddx: Penguin).

Rousseau, J. J. (1911), *Emile* [1762], trans. B. Foxley (London: Dent).

Ryle, G. (1967), 'Plato', in Edwards (1967), Vol. VI, pp. 314–33.

Skidelsky, R. (1969), *English Progressive Schools* (Harmondsworth, Mddx: Penguin).

Skilbeck, M. (ed.) (1970), *John Dewey* (London: Collier Macmillan).

Strawson, P. F. (1974), 'Imagination and perception', in P. F. Strawson, *Freedom and Resentment and Other Essays* (London: Methuen).

Taylor, C. (1975), *Hegel* (Cambridge: CUP).

Toulmin, S. (1953), *The Philosophy of Science* (London: Hutchinson).

Toulmin, S., and Goodfield, J. (1961), *The Fabric of the Heavens* (London: Hutchinson).

Toulmin, S., and Goodfield, J. (1962), *The Architecture of Matter* (London: Hutchinson).

Toulmin, S., and Goodfield, J. (1965), *The Discovery of Time* (London: Hutchinson).

Warnock, M. (1973), 'Towards a definition of quality in education', in R. S. Peters (ed.), *The Philosophy of Education* (London: OUP), pp. 112–22.

Warnock, M. (1976), *Imagination* (London: Faber).

Warnock, M. (1977), *Schools of Thought* (London: Faber).

Warnock, M. (1978), 'Educating the imagination', in G. N. Vesey (ed.), *Human Values* (Hassocks, Sussex: Harvester Press).

White, J. P. (1973), *Towards a Compulsory Curriculum* (London: Routledge & Kegan Paul).

Winch, P. (1958), *The Idea of a Social Science* (London: Routledge & Kegan Paul).

Wolheim, R. (1970), *Art and Its Objects* (Harmondsworth, Mddx: Penguin).

Index